from HABAKKUK to SARA

The Memoir
of the Reverend Stephen Szilagyi,
and the Founding of the
SARA Ministry

Edited by Arthur L. Weldy

Order this book online at www.trafford.com
or email orders@trafford.com

Most Trafford titles are also available at major online book retailers.

Note for Librarians: A cataloguing record for this book is available from Library
and Archives Canada at www.collectionscanada.ca/amicus/index-e.html

Printed in Victoria, BC, Canada.

ISBN: 978-1-4269-1103-3 (Soft)
ISBN: 978-1-4269-1105-7 (e-book)

*We at Trafford believe that it is the responsibility of us all, as both individuals
and corporations, to make choices that are environmentally and socially sound.
You, in turn, are supporting this responsible conduct each time you purchase a
Trafford book, or make use of our publishing services. To find out how you are
helping, please visit www.trafford.com/responsiblepublishing.html*

*Our mission is to efficiently provide the world's finest, most comprehensive
book publishing service, enabling every author to experience success.
To find out how to publish your book, your way, and have it available
worldwide, visit us online at www.trafford.com*

Trafford rev. 05/13/2009

Trafford
PUBLISHING® www.trafford.com

North America & international
toll-free: 1 888 232 4444 (USA & Canada)
phone: 250 383 6864 ♦ fax: 250 383 6804 ♦ email: info@trafford.com

The United Kingdom & Europe
phone: +44 (0)1865 487 395 ♦ local rate: 0845 230 9601
facsimile: +44 (0)1865 481 507 ♦ email: info.uk@trafford.com

10 9 8 7 6 5 4 3 2 1

TABLE OF CONTENTS

Introduction: The Reverend Robert Molsberry, Conference
            Minister The Ohio Conference, United Church
            of Christ   vii

Foreword: Jean Szilagyi   xi

Chapter I: The Day the Trucks Came   13

Chapter II: Return from Hell   18

Chapter III: The Russians are Coming   25

Chapter IV: Journey to a New Land   29

Chapter V: Wandering in the Wilderness   34

Chapter VI: Back to the Border   37

Chapter VII: Speaking for God   42

Chapter VIII: A Call for Help from Haiti   46

Chapter IX: Imagine Shaking Hands with the President 53

Chapter X: Miracles: Sometimes God
                 Doubles His Efforts   60

Chapter XI: God has a Sense of Humor   64

Chapter XII: The Boy with the Crooked Back   67

Chapter XIII: The Answer was at my Finger Tips   71

Chapter XIV: Miklos Arrives   75

Chapter XV: Sara is Born   79

Chapter XVI: Sara Needed Godparents   85

Chapter XVII: Hooked on Sara   91

Chapter XVIII: Random Acts of Kindness   97

Chapter XIX: Congo Comes to Conneaut   103

Chapter XX: A Children's Sermon for Adults   108

Chapter XXI: A Parable for Today:
                The Lifeguard who Wasn't Watching   113

Chapter XXII: So This is Retirement   119

Chapter XXIII ~ Epilogue: So Much for Retirement!   126

INTRODUCTION
REV. ROBERT MOLSBERRY
CONFERENCE MINISTER
OHIO CONFERENCE
UNITED CHURCH OF CHRIST

This is not a remarkable book. Stephen Szilagyi is not a remarkable wordsmith, English being his second language and all. The plot is pedantic and predictable. And there are far too many big, long unpronounceable words with far too many "z"s" and other consonants. No, in terms of its contribution to the field of literature, this is not a remarkable book at all.

But the reality described in "From Habakkuk to SARA" is indeed remarkable. Like a stained glass window, which allows a glimpse of the divine to cascade into a dark sanctuary when the sun shines just right, this book offers the reader a glimpse of a truly remarkable ministry through which God's compassion becomes concrete in our world.

The Rev. Stephen Szilagyi, who was molded by harsh wartime conditions in Hungary and then escaped Russian occupation with his father, is a story-teller. The stories he tells, when taken as a whole, illustrate not only his own history, but the history of his lifetime mission project, SARA, (*Sharing America's Resources

Abroad").Every story is a miracle: one person in need, responded to by one compassionate Pastor who builds a network of caring individuals who find that together they can respond to hundreds of persons in need with millions of dollars. Doctors are trained; clinics established; borders and boundaries are broken down; and God's work is done effectively. In spite of the number of times I've read this little book, I still find tears in my eyes at rereading some of the tales. It really is remarkable.

Steve's favorite word is "hooked". People who hear about global needs and the pathways SARA has provided to meet those needs get hooked, engaged, involved. Steve takes no credit. "I'm just a sinful man," he demurs. "To God be the Glory." Steve's enthusiasm is absolutely irresistible. Just try saying "no" to him. I dare you. SARA offers one model for people to connect with one another across the globe, and for Americans to meet glaring needs of others. This is not the model I practiced in three years with the Peace Corps in Guatemala and another three years with the Mennonite Central Committee in Nicaragua. I taught community development, empowering local people to organize to meet the needs of their neighborhoods and villages. I was not a provider of resources. But when we encountered an effective community organization that was ready to confront its local problems, we looked for funding organizations that could leverage huge improvements in community life with the investment of a few dollars. SARA is just such an organization.

It is Steve's hope, and mine as well, that "From Habakkuk to SARA" will introduce this ministry to a broader circle of friends and supporters, that the organization might be empowered through this added exposure to grow and thereby become even more effective in its outreach around the world. The Ohio Conference of the United Church of Christ stands ready to offer its structure and resources to enhance this ministry, but it really is a ministry all its own, created and sustained by the passion of its founder, the selfless commitment of the countless volunteers who have contributed to it (Steve's wife, Jean, filled 28 pages with names of significant contributors!) and blessed by a compassionate God whose will is accomplished in a mighty way through the ministry of SARA.

I recommend that you read the book, but don't stop there. After all, it's an unremarkable book. Hear Steve's enthusiasm. Let yourself get hooked. Get in touch with us. Learn more about SARA. Soon you'll be just as enthusiastic as Steve – if that's possible. And then more miracles will happen and God will be well pleased.

FOREWORD

For many years I've been urging my husband, The Reverend Stephen Szilagyi, to *"put your life and good works on paper."* His problem is that he simply "hates" computers. He tells me that he doesn't even want to be in the same room with them. Moreover, although he speaks five languages fluently, and continually amazes me by conversing in at least five more, he admits that he spells adequately *in none.* So, taking matters into my own hands I began following him around with a tape recorder, capturing every thought in his head, and then transferring them to paper in a "stream of conscience" sort of way.

Steve had only one request. He wanted any words written in this book not to concentrate on *his* life so much as the life of SARA which has been a great joy and blessing to him since he conceived it after meeting a boy with a crooked back in Hungary two decades ago. Since then, we have been astounded and overjoyed to see the concept behind SARA (Sharing America's Resources Abroad) develop into a major force for good, with operations throughout the world.

Yes, you may ask about the strange title of the book: *"From Habakkuk to SARA"*. When Reverend Steve was born in Czechoslovakia in 1934, his mother announced to his father, a Greek Catholic priest, that she had delivered a little prophet to him...not a big one such as Moses or Isaiah, but a somewhat minor one such as... perhaps...Habakkuk. And like Habakkuk, the SARA ministry which began with a very small voice, now speaks to the concerns of people all over the world – from Africa to Ukraine; Haiti to Hungary – in a very loud voice, offering hope and relief to a broken and hurting world.

It has often been said that nobody ever writes his autobiography without a lot of help from friends and family. This is particularly true of *"From Habakkuk to SARA"*. Luckily, we have a dear friend, Carol Hall, from Conneaut, Ohio, who transcribed Steve's spoken words onto paper. Lots of words and lots of paper. We also have a former parishoner in Millvale, PA who is not just a good friend, but a magna cum laude English Major Graduate from the University of Pittsburgh, with a Phi Beta Kappa key at that. Art took all the words, edited them, and boiled them down into twenty-plus chapters. And there you have it. A slim volume that encapsulates the life of a dedicated minister and of a powerful ministry that continues to expand and flourish.

I hope you enjoy this book. Perhaps you will even want to be a part of SARA which reflects not just my husband's good works, but the living Presence of Christ.

Jean Szilagyi

CHAPTER I

THE DAY THE TRUCKS CAME

"Remember now thy Creator in the days of thy youth while the evil days come not... "
Ecclesiastics 12:1 (KJV)

As a boy of ten in May, 1944, I grew up in a country at war, but gave it little thought. I knew that Hungary was allied with Germany, and, of course, there were German soldiers stationed in our town. In fact, there was an anti-aircraft gun emplacement just a block from our house. But I never saw a bomb drop from the skies, nor heard the whine of a bullet.

It was a peaceful world for children of my age. Only the grownups knew the full horror happening not more than a hundred miles away. The war seemed to have passed us by.

My home town of Munkacs is located in the foothills of the Carpathian Mountains in a region of Ukraine called Transcarpathia today, and by some as Ruthenia, depending upon their nationality. Ruthenia would be best translated in English as "little Russia." And because so many people of so many nationalities other than Russian have crossed paths here over the centuries, it's considered by many as "the other side of the mountains" depending upon which direction you are looking!

There were, indeed, many Ruthenians and their Ukrainian "cousins" in Munkacs, or Mukachevo as they called it. But there were other nationalities there as well, such as Czechs, Slovaks, Romanians, Jews, Gypsies, Germans and Hungarians. My family was Hungarian, and proud of our heritage and our unique language. Even today the region is not so much a melting pot as it is a stew which has been boiling for centuries.

The roads in Munkacs run in many directions. The region itself has had many names, and many changes of names, depending upon who conquered it at any particular time in the past. Imagine a place where my father was born and grew up in what was called the Austro-Hungarian Empire. By the time I came along, I was born in the same spot, but it was now located in Czechoslovakia! When World War II began, the region reverted to the Kingdom of Hungary which, oddly enough, was ruled by an Admiral, even though the country was land-locked.

When the Red Army stormed through the region, the region was annexed to the Soviet Union, and I found myself going to a school officially located in Russia. In later years when I returned to Munkacs, it lay within the borders of The Republic of Ukraine. The land never moved; only the political borders. Armies have fought over it since the beginning of time, and geography has been its great misfortune.

Friends of my age felt little misfortune in the Spring of 1944. We wandered the woods unafraid, fished in the river, played football (soccer) in the schoolyard and squirmed on Sunday mornings during mass. I should say that the other boys squirmed, while I, the son of the Greek Catholic priest, had to maintain a very stiff and proper posture as an example. This was at the command of my mother, who was not to be trifled with.

Before we go further, I assure you that Greek Catholic priests were allowed, and indeed, encouraged to marry at that time. As a priest, my father was respected and admired throughout the city, and I was never ashamed to be known as "the priest's son."

In that day and age, children were sent out of the house in the morning and were free to roam without adult supervision until they got hungry or it got dark. On a particularly beautiful morning in early May-- it was Saturday, my favorite day of the week-- the people of Munkacs were gathering for market day in the town square. I cared not much for the market, and beat a path through the barley fields up into the woods, the foothills of the Carpathian mountains, toward a stream where I knew I might catch a crayfish or a lizard or two, or perhaps some tadpoles.

At a point on the path, high up in the mountain meadows where the deeper woods began, I saw an old fellow from the village, hunched and gray, carrying a large bag over his back. He was an old Hungarian gentleman named Kecskemety, with many missing teeth, and somewhat hard of hearing. He greeted me in Hungarian as I raised my cap. When I think of it now, I doubt he ever saw a doctor, let alone a dentist or a specialist of any kind. We Americans take those things for granted. To our credit, we take great care to see that our children are healthy and well-fed. We make sure their teeth are straight and that they receive immunizations for a multitude of childhood diseases.

Then, and even today in eastern Europe and other parts of the world, medical care is often a luxury, particularly for the very old and the very young. Crooked teeth, cleft palates, curvature of the spine, "lazy eye", club feet – all of these still abound in rural areas as well as larger cities. Retarded children then, and sometimes even now, were often hidden within the homes of the peasants because they were "bad luck" or perhaps from the religious conviction that someone must have sinned a great deal to bring this kind of trouble upon the family.

The old fellow seemed to be "up in years" to me, but I doubt he was more than sixty at the time. He lived, alone, in a small shed, warmed with a wood fire in the winter, but he was always busy, always cheerful, and on that particularly beautiful morning in May he delighted in showing me some of the herbs and fine mushrooms he gathered for market day. Many of them would turn up on my mother's table. My father said the old fellow knew a secret place to find them.

That morning in May, I very politely asked the old man about this secret place. He winked at me and said: "If you want fine mushrooms, you must go where sheep have been. You know, boy, where they do their business. Yes, "he laughed, " that's the secret."

This part of the woods was high above the town, and in the distance, we heard a low rumble, growing louder, and saw a large brown cloud appearing above the main road. Kecskemety put his hand over his eyes and told me that there must be a lot of traffic heading into town.. Something was happening that neither he nor I had ever seen before. Whatever it was, it was raising a lot of dust, and I must run and see it, leaving the old man in my own dust.

When I reached the market square about half an hour later, I looked down the street to the quarter where the Jewish people lived. I realize now that it was a ghetto where all the Jews from miles around were confined within a few blocks.

Although I was not aware of it at the time, the Jewish Community in Munkacs was large and flourishing before the war. A rabbinical college founded by the noted Rabbi Chaim Elazan Spira drew scholars from all over Europe. The Rabbi was highly respected by the international Jewish community and by the gentile world as well. He wrote many books, and important people like President Benes of Czechoslovakia and Queen Wilhelmina of The Netherlands, sometimes stopped by to talk with him. He died shortly before the war, and by 1944 his college was closed and his followers were trapped in the Ghetto and wore yellow stars on their coats.

As I looked down the street, I saw a long line of grey German army trucks and groups of people being herded into them. And not just by German soldiers, but by some of our own policemen as well. Old people and young; men, women, and children as well. Some were sick and crippled, and even the cripples were hoisted up and dropped into the trucks along with the others.

I asked the man beside me what was happening. "They've come for the Jews," he said. "They're taking them away to work for them." "But who's taking them?", I asked. "The Germans are in charge now", said the man. "Even Horthy is afraid of them." I knew that Admiral Horthy was the Regent of Hungary or something like that. And if he was afraid, I realized that I should be afraid as well.

Another man said: "They say they're taking them to work in the East, but I notice that they're only allowed to take one bag of clothes. What does that tell you?"

The work was done quickly and brutally, and one after another, the fully loaded trucks sped away as fast as they had come.

I asked my father that question again when I reached our house: "Where are they taking them?" He gathered my Mother and me close to him in the kitchen. and I remember him telling us that these were bad times, terrible times. He told us that the Lord has kept us safe thus far, and we must depend upon Him to keep it so…and, he added, we must pray for those who have been taken away to only God knows where."

"They even took cripples," I thought. "What kind of work could they do?"

CHAPTER II

RETURN FROM HELL

"For a small moment have I forsaken thee: but with great mercies will I will gather thee."
Isaiah 54: 7 (KJV)

Forty years later, I thought of the day when the trucks came to Munkacs as I talked to Mr. Kovar, the proprietor of a small hotel in Atlantic City, New Jersey – now the site of a parking lot for a Casino.

Two sweet and very sprightly sisters in my congregation in Millvale, PA, invited my wife and I to spend the weekend with them at this little hotel close to the Boardwalk, and we were delighted to be their guests. They were radio performers in the early 1930's, and had visited the hotel each summer since. Although it was now in the mid 1980's, the hotel had in many ways not changed appreciably. The rooms were very small, and the floors had a noticeable tilt due to warping. Everybody said it was due to the "salt water."

The "first floor" was the registration lobby and lounge, with wicker chairs (many times painted) and large vases of artificial flowers. A restaurant on that floor had long since ceased to function. The sisters told us that the food was excellent and plentiful "before the war". If you went fishing, they said, and you brought your catch to the kitchen, it would be prepared for your dinner later that evening. An upstairs porch featured a row of comfortable rocking chairs.

There were two elevators. One went directly from the lobby to the top, fourth floor. The other was located on the back side of the hotel and descended into a shower and dressing room in the basement. Beach goers were not permitted in the lobby with bathing suits. Gentility was preserved by taking the "beach elevator" and walking out the side entrance and under the Boardwalk to the beach.

Mr Kovar was a small man, but stocky and broad-shouldered, with powerful arms. He was just a few years older than me, and spoke with a heavy middle European accent that was readily understandable to me.

During the summer months – the "Season" as they called it-- Mr Kovar came by the hotel at supper time, and stayed through the night, sleeping on a sofa in the registration area, guarding the door and opening it to guests who straggled in during the night. Casino gambling was still relatively new in the city, and the two sisters were inveterate and unrepentant slot machine addicts who arrived "home" most often after midnight.

Mr Kovar always greeted them with good humor as he unlocked the door and asked about their luck, which was never very good. He was pleased to have two very well-dressed and well-paying guests, and they were pleased to have someone "sit up" for them each evening.

Kovar's wife, in contrast to him, was a tall, dark-haired, attractive woman about his same age. One knew that she had been a beauty in her day by her lovely olive skin, large dark eyes, and the certain way she carried herself. She came on duty at 6:00am, made breakfast for him, and sent him home. Thereafter, she worked until 6:00pm, performing such duties as manager, housemaid, room clerk, accountant, and anything else that was necessary for the general upkeep of the hotel and its forty or more guests. She usually left at 6:30pm for their home in Margate, but not before making a hearty supper for her husband. She seemed to take all of her meals "on the run." She thought nothing of the hardest kind of work.

When I was first introduced to them, Kovar had just finished supper, and his wife was filling him in on some of the events of the day, and what he might expect that evening. They began in English, and then, when there were some confidential things to discuss, they passed over into Hungarian. I said very quickly in Hungarian: "Excuse me. There are things that you might not wish to discuss in front of me. I can understand everything you say, and I'm a Pastor," I laughed.

Kovar was electrified and began to speak excitedly in Hungarian. "You speak like we did at home," he said. " Where are you from?" "Munkacs", I said. Kovar took my hand. "I lived not twenty miles away. In Kisvarda. During the war. Until they took us away". (Somehow God "connects all the dots". Today Jeannie and I have a home just a few kilos away from Kisvarda which we use as a base for SARA activities in Eastern Europe each summer).

"I was just a boy," I said, "but I remember the day they took the Jews away from Munkacs."

"It was the same time they took us from Kisvarda," he said. "In the Spring of 1944." Kovar paused for a moment, then continued: "The ladies told me that you are a man of God, Szilagyi. A Pastor."

"Yes, and my father was a Greek Catholic Priest... in Munkacs."

Kovar pulled me to the side. "Then you know what happened at Auschwitz, because Auschwitz is where they took us. First by truck to Debrecen, and then by train, right into the concentration camp."

"We thought you were being taken to the east to work," I said, " but what we saw later in the newsreels and when we read the books after the war, we only realized how horrifying it must have been."

Kovar began to speak in a torrent of Hungarian: " I have never spoken about it before. Not even to my children. Especially not to my two girls. Not for forty years. It was so terrible that I don't even dream about it. I just closed my mind to it. But I can talk with you. You were there to see it happen, and you are a man of God. And besides that, we speak the same language. I need to talk to someone who remembers. It's been forty years, and people forget." As his eyes misted over, he began his story of what happened during that week in May when the deportations began while I watched as a child. "They took us by truck to Debrecen, then loaded us on cattle cars with little windows and not much air to breathe. It took us many days to reach Auschwitz."

"When we got there, the train went all the way into the camp", he said. "While some of the German soldiers stood guard, others began unloading the cars, using dogs and rifle butts to herd us forward and to separate mothers from their children. Women were screaming. Old people and the smallest children were quickly separated by force from the group.

One of the guards who was helping the soldiers looked familiar to me -- but for what reason I do not know. Anyway, he said quietly to me in Hungarian: 'If you can run at all, run to the right' I immediately sprang forward, joining those who, I found, were to be saved from immediate death."

"Later," Kovar continued, "I became one of those guards who helped separate the weaker ones from the strong ones. Those who were sick or old, or deformed, or impaired in any way, were immediately taken away to the gas chambers...within minutes."

He could barely speak.

"I was made to do terrible things, Szilagyi. We were worked eleven hours a day and lived nearly 500 to one barrack, without heat and very little food. Food you wouldn't have given to the pigs. The places swarmed with lice, and worse." Many were sick, with diarrhea...."

He hesitated, for a moment, while his wife walked away from us. She could not bear to hear it.

"You know, Szilagyi, I have never even spoken to anyone about this until now. Because, you see, I had to do terrible things, and I knew God would never forgive me. I herded people that I knew into the gas chambers. He was in tears now. " Then I had to pull them out and take them to the furnaces. God will never forgive me," he repeated.

"Only this one thing got me through," he continued. "I was pushing this naked old man along to the gas chamber, you see, and I whispered to him: 'Forgive me.' He knew full well what was happening, although some of the women and younger children didn't seem to. He looked me full in the face and answered quietly, 'You must live to tell them what they did to us here.' Then he squeezed my arm and was herded with the others into the Brausebad, the shower room.

"Somehow that gave me the strength to go on, Szilagyi, but I still wonder if God can ever forgive me. And I wonder why He saved me and let the others die, and then allowed me to return from hell."

I answered him the best I could: "God has already forgiven you, Kovar. You have already paid the price."

He ended with tears streaming down his cheeks. "What they did to us Jews was horrible. What they did to others—especially the Gypsies, I cannot even speak about. My wife is a Romanian Gypsy, Szilagyi."

The story of Mr Kovar was not finished on that day in 1984. Some years later –Jack Lawson, the son of one of the sisters who stayed at Mr Kovar's hotel, was visiting Atlantic City in July, 2006, and parked in the lot next to the casino. To his amazement, the little man who now controlled the entrance gate and collected the money, was none other then Mr. Kovar. He had to be in his late seventies, or even eighty. But he recognized Mr. Lawson immediately, because he had often accompanied his mother and aunt to Atlantic City in years gone by. Kovar called for his wife on his cell phone, and she quickly appeared with some coffee and sweet roles. It was a very sentimental meeting. Their teen age girls were now grown-up with families of their own. The "Lawson Sisters" had long since passed away.

Mr. Lawson told me later that Kovar asked about the kind Hungarian Pastor he had met years ago, and was gratified to know that he was doing just fine in Ohio. And then, Mrs. Kovar said, with a small grin on her still-beautiful face: "You know that Mr. Kovar is no longer kosher!"

Kovar interrupted and quickly explained: "I had a heart operation not long ago, and they give me a pig valve! But I'm still surviving," he laughed.

Although I have not been to Atlantic City since that weekend in 1984, I pray God that Mr. Kovar is still working at surviving on his little patch of parking lot. Think of it. The whole Nazi Empire has disintegrated: all of its leaders; its guns and tanks, airplanes and ships; all of the SS and the murderous guards. All of it gone to dust. And in a sense, the old man who walked naked into the gas chamber challenging Kovar to "live to tell others" remains the victor.

The picture of deformed children being hoisted into the trucks and the horror of thinking about what happened to them in Auschwitz has remained in my mind. Although I was not aware of it, God was even then preparing me for a mission which was to come later in my life. A mission which would be called SARA.

CHAPTER III

THE RUSSIANS ARE COMING

"For there they that carried us away captive required of us a song."
Psalm 137:3 (KJV)

I realized after I talked with Mr. Kovar that just a few miles and a few years had separated me from the hell in which he lived during those last months of World War II.

As for me, a schoolboy of ten, a relative calm had fallen in Munkacs after the Red Army quickly overran our region and moved swiftly toward Budapest. Many of the people of Munkacs had awaited the arrival of the Russians with horror. They knew from returning Hungarian soldiers about the atrocities committed in Russia by the SS, and they expected the same in Hungary. After all, Hungary was technically an ally of Germany.

Hitler had ordered that eastern Hungary be defended at all costs, and the German High Command ignored all pleas for surrender. While the Red Army spared Munkacs from the worst of it, they besieged Budapest from October, 1944 until the following February. Over one hundred thousand civilians died. It was not the first, nor would it be the last time that Russian soldiers slaughtered Hungarians.

Some in Munkacs had been communists since the days when a man named Bela Kun, a short-lived communist dictator, held power briefly after World War I.

They looked forward to welcoming the Russians as "liberators", and although they represented a minority of Hungarians, it was not long before they grabbed control of the government and held it in a death grip for the next forty years.

As for the rest of us, including my family, we simply waited to see what we would need to do to survive. I knew little of the rape and plunder which the Red Army inflicted on most of the rest of the country and particularly Budapest, the capital. For children of my age, it was an exciting time to be alive. In the wake of several skirmishes in and around our city, there was a vast reservoir of war material that we boys discovered and played with, including broken rifles, spent bullets, artillery shells and even some live hand grenades.

Much of the stuff had been dumped in the river by fleeing Germans, and we had a grand time swimming in that area and examining our "catch" I found some dynamite in a small box one day and did my best to make it blow up. I threw rocks at it and even tried to set it on fire. Only God knows why I didn't blow myself up.

I nearly frightened my mother to death as I brought pieces of weapons and ammunition to her doorstep. One day I walked into the kitchen with the remains of a "panzer-faust" which is a hand-held anti-tank weapon. Somehow we survived.

The schools reopened, and I prepared to enter what would be the Fifth Grade in an American school system. When I arrived at the familiar school building, there were strange new teachers, and a fierce-looking school superintendent who stood atop the steps leading into the school, with hands crossed.

We were assembled in our classrooms, and the superintendent visited each of them. I don't remember his exact words, but they went something like this:

"You are no longer Hungarians, Slovaks, Czechs, Ukrainians, or anything else. From now on, you are citizens of the Mighty Soviet Union of Federated Socialist Republics." "There are 200 million of us," he roared, "and our Motherland is the largest and most powerful country in the world. We have destroyed our enemies at an enormous cost. Over 20 million of our people have perished to preserve your freedom. We would have been slaves if the Germans had conquered us, but we are victorious. And you are very lucky to become a part of a great nation."

He said little or nothing about the contribution which the British and the Americans had made in the war.

"From now on," he continued, "we speak Russian in our classes. Don't worry. Russian is a beautiful language, and you will learn it quickly. It is a strong language," he said, "and when you speak it, you must bring it up from here." He pointed to his chest. "And not just from your mouth."

"Now," he continued "we will start immediately by singing the national anthem of the Soviet Motherland!" He passed out words on a sheet. And so we sang, from our chests, and at the top of our voices:

"Russia, our beloved land…"

Americans might think that this was totally confusing to children our age, but living in Munkacs, we were quite familiar with speakers of Slavic languages such as Czech, Slovak, Ukrainian, Polish or Serbian. These languages are similar to Russian, and speakers of any of these tongues can fairly well understand all of the familiar words.

Hungarian does not fit into that category. None of the words in the Hungarian vocabulary match any word in any other language. Our Magyar forefathers rode onto the Hungarian Plain from somewhere far to the East long before recorded history. The language they spoke and their food was different from anything around them. In any case, most Hungarians were proud of their "difficult-to-learn" language, and found it useful to carry two or more additional languages in their pockets.

In our new lessons, our history books no longer spoke about Prince Arpad who crossed the Carpathians and settled in Hungary around 900AD, or good Saint Stephen who converted Hungary to Christianity around the year 1000. We didn't hear about those exciting Huns who carried raw meat under their saddles for supper.

Instead we were taught history from the Russian point of view, with great emphasis on the wickedness of the Hapsburgs and the Tsars. Our heroes were to be Lenin, Marx, and the rest of the dry-as-dust proletarians who rescued us all from the rotten capitalists.

And so, within a few weeks, we all became good little Russians. We continued to speak Hungarian at home, of course, and my father always reminded me that I was not a Russian nor ever would be. But of course, we were not permitted to speak of this in school. At the time, I thought that learning Russian was a great waste of time. But God had plans that I had yet to understand. My Russian served me well when I later served as an interpreter with the United States Army, and again when I visited hospitals and orphanages in Ukraine on behalf of the SARA ministry.

How I became an American, after being born a Czech, entering school as a Hungarian, and finishing it as a Russian is something which would play out within the next few years. God seemed to be using me as a soccer ball. And what started the ball rolling was a political development in Prague in 1948...

CHAPTER IV

JOURNEY TO A NEW LAND

"Now the Lord had said unto Abram, Get thee out of thy country and from thy kindred...unto a land that I will show thee" (KJV)

While I was becoming a "good little Russian" in the elementary school I attended, our little region of the world was fast becoming a Soviet military bridgehead created to assure communist domination of all Central Europe.

My father was an extremely intelligent man and he saw the misery that was coming. Although he was a priest, he was also a "drinking man" -- but not an alcoholic -- instantly sober when he arrived inside our home. I suspect it was a "disguise" in many ways to protect us from the KGB. One could be intelligent under Communism, but not TOO intelligent.

He preached in several small churches in the area, and taught in a small business school. Before the war, he had obtained a doctorate in law from the University of Debrecen in Hungary, and he had been able to travel to the Sorbonne in Paris to study. So he was a very educated man, and worldly wise for being a priest. His voice was very loud, and he was, to be honest, quite stubborn and aggressive. He did not hesitate to use the switch on me

We moved quietly from Munkacs during that time, to a little village where my aunt lived, across the border in Czechoslovakia, which at that time was still free. It would not stay free for very long. The communists were already agitating for political control although they were a small minority in the country. And after all, they had the power of the Red Army behind them, just across the border.

My life would soon take a dramatic turn, and it all began on a bus ride with my aunt. She had an errand to run, and happily, I was able to go with her. I remember her remarking to a neighbor who was sitting across from us about the latest news that Jan Masaryk, son of the first president of Czechoslovakia, had fallen out of a window in Prague, and died. The neighbor man said: "He didn't fall. He was pushed!"

Someone on the bus had overheard him, and two stops later he was arrested and taken from the bus. This is how I remember the beginning of the Communist takeover in Czechoslovakia. And this is when my father determined that we must get out of the country into a new land. It was a message which was as clear to him as God's message to Abraham in the Book of Genesis. My father determined that I would live free, even if it meant leaving my homeland and my family. And that's exactly what happened.

My father had a sense of urgency because, as a priest, he could feel himself being "observed". There was a man in our village who was a "nobody" before the Communists took over. Suddenly, he revealed himself as a party member and immediately took a great interest in my father's comings and goings. He confronted him in the street one day and threatened him with the words: "I know you. I know where you come from! I said 'hello' to you in the street one day, and you didn't even answer me back!" Thus spoke the proletariat to a man of intelligence and culture. Who knew what would happen next.

What happened next was the arrest of Josef Cardinal Mindszenty, the Roman Catholic Primate of Hungary. Hungary, and all the world, was shocked when he was sent to prison for "treason." After all, he had been imprisoned by the Nazis for several years during the war. Now he was to spend twenty-three years of persecution, suffering and enforced isolation before being released in 1971. The Communists had declared war on the church, and my father was a priest. We had to go. And quickly.

(Little did I think then that one day many years later, I would be on the same platform as Cardinal Mindszenty and participating with one of the the welcoming speeches during his tour of the United States in the early 1970's).

Luckily, my father had gone to high school with the man who had become the Communist Party Secretary for the region. He immediately came to our rescue, but he reminded us that his days might be numbered as well.

One night, with little more than the shirts on our backs, my father and I left home. My mother knew that she would not be able to make such a trip as lay ahead of us. It was a tearful goodbye. After all, I was only fourteen at the time, and still "a little boy" to her.

We traveled south by train and bus from our town in Czechoslovakia for several days, toward the Austrian border. We stayed overnight in a small hotel near Bratislava, and on Sunday morning, armed with fishing poles made of sticks, string, and small hooks, we walked toward a canal on the Danube, in a swampy area, pretending to be on a fishing expedition. We were about two kilometers from the Austrian border. It was a park-like setting, and several families were picnicking there.

Suddenly, a young Border Guard appeared from the woods and came up quickly to us. He pointed to the trees and said: "The border is over there. Don't go beyond those woods or you might get in trouble." Was it a warning, or an invitation to leave?

Only God knows. His angels come in different disguises. After the guard walked away, we waited for about an hour, and then scrambled toward the part of the woods where the guard told us specifically not to go.

We had intentionally worn light clothing and carried no baggage. Now it was getting colder, and I shivered in my small jacket.

When we got to one of the canal locks, we walked through water up to our knees. Shoes and all. Then we started running until we came to another wooded area where we heard voices. Two border guards walked past us as we hid in the bushes and sat down on the ground nearby... not twenty feet away. So we lay there, very quietly, and held our breath.

It seemed like an eternity. I remember whispering to my father that I had to go to the bathroom, and he told me that if I had ever held it, to hold it now! We lay there until they left, and even then, waited until it got dark before we left the shelter of the trees.

We ran across many fields and crossed several small creeks. Suddenly, just beyond a small farm house, we saw a paved highway. My father said that a road like this could only lead to Vienna, which he reckoned to be about sixty kilometers or about forty miles away. When we saw car lights, we hid behind buildings, or in the woods along side the road. I still held tightly to my fishing stick.

At some point during the night I told my father that I could not go on. So he gave me his jacket with the sleeves rolled up, and I slept in a ditch for about two hours. Then we continued. We knew we were in Austria because the road signs were in German – but Russian-controlled Austria. As the dawn came, and the morning lightened, once again we pretended to be just a father and son going fishing...or coming from fishing, whichever! My father had only a small hard roll and a triangular shaped piece of yellow cheese which we ate while we lay in a ditch near the road.

My father spoke fluent German, and had no trouble convincing some farmers and others who passed by on foot that we were what we seemed to be. We walked on during the next day and into the next.

The countryside became "busier", and finally we arrived on the edge of Vienna -- we could read the sign pointing to Wien-- where there was a check-point and Russian border guards. Vienna was divided into four sectors: French, British, American, and of course, Russian. To get to the American sector of the city, we had to somehow get past the Russian soldier who was stationed next to a high wall. I quietly asked my father: "What do we do now?" After all, we had no papers whatsoever. He said to me: "Son, I am deaf and dumb, and you don't talk!"

Of course, I still had on my light jacket and my fishing rod, and must have looked like something out of a story by Mark Twain. The young guard simply looked us over and waved us on. Incredible! We walked into the American Zone of Vienna. Without saying a word. God was with us. I have no doubt. Whether the guard was another of God's angels, I do not know. After walking nearly forty miles, however, I was totally exhausted, and my feet sore and swollen. Every step was an effort, and I was almost hit with a car as we crossed into American-controlled Vienna because I simply couldn't run to get out of the way. The American government had set up a relief agency for political escapees, and soon had us set up in a dormitory. They gave us hot coffee and rolls, and we slept the clock around. An American Major visited us and gave me six Hershey bars. It was truly manna from heaven. The chocolate tasted so good that I would take just a small bite and slosh it around my mouth, just letting it melt by itself. We were almost free...but not quite.

CHAPTER V

WANDERING THROUGH THE WILDERNESS

"But God led the people about, through the way of the wilderness..."
Exodus 13:18 (KJV)

Freedom seemed close at hand, but God kept my father and I wandering for the next four years, much as the Hebrew Children wandered in the wilderness some 5,000 years before.

The problem was that we were in the American Sector of Vienna, but Vienna itself was an island in the midst of the Soviet Occupation Zone. The French and American Occupation Zones were many miles away. We could not stay here forever, and to "break-out" would entail as many dangers, if not more, than we had already encountered. But my father was determined that I should be free, and although he had no set plan, he trusted to God to bring us through.

Since we had no passports – only some useless documents that identified us as foreigners-- we were constantly being stopped and checked and re-checked. Once, we were taken off a train, arrested and spent several days in jail, behind locked doors awaiting an uncertain fate. I was still a boy the time, and very emotional about being handled as though we were criminals. Our food was meager, with meals often consisting of simply bread and margarine. For whatever reason, we were finally released to an American official -- probably a CIA Agent – who interrogated us and told us that it would be nearly impossible for us to escape from the American Sector, through the Russian Zone, into one of the Allied zones. The trains were being watched very carefully, he said, and we would be turned back again and again because we had no papers…or perhaps worse.

Like a gift from heaven, some church officials gave us some money – about 700 shillings, which was a lot of money at that time. I don't know what would have happened to us if we hadn't received this blessing. But even 700 shillings would not last very long. We tried taking the trains nearly every day, hoping to reach the American Zone, but were always turned back. Once, we actually made it through the Russian Zone and reached the border of the French Zone. My father thought we had a real advantage because he spoke flawless French. But the French authorities turned us away at their border and told us: "You go back where you came from. We have enough refugees in the French Zone" They put us on another train gong in the opposite direction, We went one stop, and got off to an uncertain future in the middle of the rail yard.

God had a plan, and it finally materialized in the rail yard in the form of a freight train with a big locomotive chugging slowly in the direction we wanted to go. We climbed aboard, hiding in one of the freight cars. The train traveled all night, stopping just once for an inspection. Luckily, we were hidden well, even as flashlights probed into every corner of the car. In the morning, we jumped from the train as it slowly pulled into the railyard in Innsbruck, French Zone. Out of the hands of the communists. Free at last.

Because my father was a priest, we were welcomed into a Capuchin monastery in the city, where we would spend the next four years living in a small cell with two beds.

We had no sooner settled ourselves in the monastery, however, when I began to have "funny feelings." I even began to hallucinate. I was examined in the monastery clinic, and my father took me to a hospital where a nurse examined me again and diagnosed me immediately. "He has diphtheria," she said. My little sister, Nathalie, had died of diphtheria when she was just four, so of course I started to cry. At age 14, it's a very traumatic thing to face death. But childhood deaths in that part of Europe were common, and expected. Families were large, and it was taken for granted that two or three children would be taken quite early in life.

God proceeded to offer me another miracle. The doctor who was assigned to me said to my father: "You're very lucky today. "I have a small dose left of penicillin, a new miracle drug. We'll see what happens."

So I was injected, and they put me in a contagious disease ward. There were four of us in one of those small rooms: myself, and three adult men, each with a contagious disease of one kind or another. We were to spend several weeks together. Needless to say, the days passed very slowly.

The hospital's morgue was in the building next to us. One morning there was an accident in the city during some kind of military exercise, and several soldiers were killed. I watched as they carried the shrouded bodies, stained in blood, into the death room.

Death was a constant companion with me during those days that went by so slowly and painfully. And I wondered: "What good can God make of all of this?"

CHAPTER VI

BACK TO THE BORDER

"And Isaiah said…shall the shadow go forward ten degrees, or go back ten degrees?"
2Kings 20:9 (KJV)

The days passed slowly in the hospital, and little by little I began to regain my strength.

I remember walking feebly out of the hospital one morning with my father, very thin and very pale, blinded by the sunshine which rarely found its way into my hospital room.

When I thought about this experience in my younger years, the initial thought that came to mind was: "Why did God do this to me? What good could come from all of that misery" As an adult, now, with many years of experience helping crippled and impaired children through the SARA program, I realize that God had been putting me through a kind of "basic training" for the work which lay ahead. He was showing me the intense mental and spiritual anguish which children suffer at the same time as they experience physical pain. I can more readily and easily relate to them now because I experienced it myself.

My father was there for me in my long and harrowing trip that led us to freedom. Without his stubborn determination and aggressiveness (which I had so often resented when I was younger, and even later in life), I could never have made it this far. On that fine day, after weeks of confinement, we walked together through the gates of the hospital and back to the monastery where my life began again.

In the three years we remained in Innsbruck, I was able to attend a high school (gymnasium as it is called in Europe) set up by displaced Ukrainians. It was a fine school, and later, I managed to attend university-level classes in a college which they also maintained.

Our luck began to change. God smiled providentially on us once more, and with great rejoicing, my father and I received information that we were being sponsored for emigration to the United States by a Greek Catholic priest friend in Newark, New Jersey. We got bits and pieces of news from Czechoslovakia and were pleased to know that my Mother was living with relatives and doing well. So we left the old world and flew to the new. We arrived in the United States on November 24, 1952, and settled down in the Promised Land. I was eighteen, and I was free.

But God had another trick up his sleeve for me, and a few months later, I was back in Germany at a border crossing in the Russian Zone.

How did that happen? I had reached the "promised land" and enjoyed it for just a few months before being returned to a place that I had just escaped from.

Well, it seems that during a conflict or war, a foreigner who enlists in the United States Army can apply for US citizenship after ninety days service. Within a few weeks of arriving in the United States, I enlisted and found myself in basic training. Compared to what I had already endured, it was "a piece of cake." Soon I proudly, and happily, swore allegiance to my new country.

Our unit, the 47th Infantry Division, was scheduled to ship off to Korea. However, the armistice signed at Panmunjon, Korea, ended the fighting, and I was sent, instead, to military police training in Camp Gordon, Georgia.

Upon completion of my training, I was flown to Germany – not all that far from Innsbruck where I had spent the previous four years -- where I found myself as an American GI serving as a Russian interpreter. God had prepared me well in my little school in Munkacs. What irony, to find myself once again facing Russian border guards, but this time from the American side of the fence.

Much like Vienna, Berlin at that time was an island administered by the Americans, British, French and Russians. Around this "island city" was the Russian Sector of control. Berlin lay about 110 miles inside the Sector, and my job was to coordinate the inspection of freight as well as passenger trains that ran from Berlin in the American Zone, across the Russian Zone, and into the American Sector of Germany.

We got along well enough with the Russian soldiers and border guards who were our own age. We even had friendly conversations with them. When the trains coming out of Berlin stopped at the Russian border, I accompanied an American officer into the control office and reported in Russian as to how many cars there were on the train, and the manifest for each of them. Normally, after some small talk, the train was on its way again within a few minutes. If the Russians were in a bad mood, it would leave in an hour or two.

I identified the Russian officers as: "the friendly one", "the grouchy one", etc. Surprisingly, the "friendly one" confronted me one day with much ranting and raving about anti-Russian propaganda which he found taped to one of the freight cars. My response was returned in anger: "Nothing of that sort was on the train," I shouted in Russian, "and we have not gotten on or off this train since it left Berlin. Apparently one of your own people did this. See for yourself, and don't bother us with this!"

He answered meekly: "You're probably right."

In another incident, a Russian Major met our train. "I want you to open this car", he said, "pointing to one which had been diplomatically sealed in Berlin. A friend of mine who was a corporal, and who could also speak Russian fluently, pointed his gun at the Major and said loudly: "If you make one move to try to open that door, I will shoot you dead as a door nail." Then he added: "If you don't want to find yourself in Siberia, you had better let this thing go right now."

The Russian Major made a couple of grunts, and walked away.

The thing I quickly learned about dealing with the Russians, or any "bad guys", is that you have to pass along your instructions from a position of strength. Our government tended to "pussy foot around" when it came to dealing with Communists or other dictators. The Communists would always say: "If you do this or that, we will start another war." They needed no provocation for starting a war. They would have invented something if they had wanted to start a war.

Their patron saint, Lenin, had warned them that anyone who starts a conflict with the West and who is not absolutely sure of victory, is good for nothing. In other words, if you made such a foolish mistake, you would pay the price. If you understood that philosophy, then you knew exactly how to deal with them.

My military career was pleasant enough as I "rode the rails" back and forth between Frankfurt and Berlin. I made friends with several of the Russian soldiers who we met each time we passed through the Russian corridor. I started a conversation with one of the soldiers named Basil, and we talked about where we were from, and all of that kind of stuff. One afternoon I said: "Do you smoke? Would you like some American cigarettes?" The Russian soldiers were chopping up tobacco roots (not leaves) at that time, and rolling them in newspaper.

He answered with the English equivalent of : "Gee, I would appreciate that very much. But the officers are watching. So when the train leaves, could you just drop a pack on the tracks. I'll watch where it falls and then pick it up after the train leaves." I made it a practice to do just that, and we became firm friends.

Shortly after this, the Russians got nasty and closed the rail corridor. They kept open just one highway into Berlin, and all traffic flowed through it. Cars and trucks were often lined up for miles leading to the checkpoint.

One day, a friend of mine who had to drive a rickety old '42 Chevy -- held together pretty much with wire – found himself at the very end of the line. Ahead of him were American colonels, government officials, and diplomats: all waiting to pass through the checkpoint at a snail's pace. Basil, my Russian soldier friend, recognized the driver of the Chevy and asked him: "How is Steve?" Following this, he pulled the car out of line, looked quickly over his papers, and sent this corporal on his way while the higher officers and diplomats waited and fumed.

I can tell you honestly that this is the way it works in Eastern Europe. It's not what you represent, but **who you know** in the system. I found it very helpful in the future when I had to haggle a bit even to ship medical equipment and supplies across the borders as part of SARA.

My service years passed by quickly, and soon I found myself boarding a plane for "home", and wondering what path God would open up to me in my adopted country. I even began to think about who I might find as a bride.

41

CHAPTER VII

SPEAKING FOR GOD

"And Moses said unto the Lord, O my Lord, I am not eloquent, neither heretofore, nor since thou hast spoken unto thy servant: but I am slow of speech and of a slow tongue."
Exodus 4:10 (KJV)

While God had given me a gentle nudge now and again, he gave me a decided PUSH when I returned home from Europe after my tour of duty, and was honorably discharged from the service.

During the time I was away, my father had experienced many problems. For one thing, the Greek Catholic Church in America did not recognize married priests as it did in Europe. He could not possibly serve in any church within the United States. While I was away, he lived on what little he could earn as a janitor in a Hungarian Reformed Church in New York City, pastored by the Reverend Imre Kovacs.

My father still considered himself as a man of God, and after much deliberation and many prayers, he decided to become a member of the Reformed Church, and to apply for the ministry. We had many Protestants in our family (Hungary is about 1/3 Protestant, and 2/3 Roman Catholic), and it seemed a natural way to serve the Lord considering his new set of circumstances.

He was quickly embraced by his Hungarian Calvinist "brothers" and began preaching in a little church in New Jersey where he was greatly admired for his strong delivery. He had a deep baritone voice which carried to every corner of every church he preached in. But a great tragedy was about to engulf us and to change the direction of his life and mine.

It started with a series of sore throats, which he quickly waved off. But then it got worse. After an extensive examination by a specialist, it was discovered that he had cancer of the larynx. It was moving quickly now and would surely render him almost speechless during the remaining years of his life. He took the diagnosis bravely, but he had great compassion for his little church and how he could continue to serve it. After many prayers on his part, he decided that someone would have to assist him at his little church. And that someone was me!

"But Father," I said, "I don't know anything about preaching. I wouldn't know where to begin."

My father assured me that he could teach me all I needed to know. Of course, I was reluctant and unwilling, but my father had done so much for me that I felt it impossible not to attempt to help him. It seems that I had inherited his strong voice, and with some advice about projection, that part worked itself out. But I was completely unsure about how to conduct a service, and a Reformed one at that.

He typed the sermon and outlined the order of worship on paper. He marked in black those places where I should speak, and in red those places where I should do gestures, or other things in the course of the worship service. Even so, it seemed impossible for us to manage it.

In those first weeks of speaking for my father, I wondered why God would choose me of all people to be a minister, and why he would choose such a circuitous path to do it. My father sent me to the Book of Exodus where Moses made the same statement to God as I did to my father. The words are in Exodus 4; 10-12. *"Oh my Lord, I am not eloquent, neither heretofore nor since thou hast spoken to thy servant, but I am slow of speech and of a slow tongue."*

The Lord answered: "Who made man's mouth, or who maketh the dumb, or deaf, or the seeing, or the blind? Have not I, the Lord? Now therefore go, and I will be with thy mouth, and teach thee what thou shalt say."

I certainly don't compare myself to Moses, nor my father to God. But I think God gives us examples from time to time of what he wants us to do with our lives, and most importantly his promise to "back us up" when we speak for him. And my father must have learned the lesson well before I did. Somehow we managed, and successfully at that. As time went on, I told him that I wanted to formally become a member of the Reformed Church as well, and with that in mind I attended the nearby Princeton Seminary, then on to Oberlin Graduate School, and finally the Evangelical Congregational School of Theology in Myerstown, PA.

While all of this was going on, God put me in touch with a student nurse while I was having a short stay at the hospital for a minor operation. She turned out to be a devout Roman Catholic and told me in no uncertain terms that she could never marry a Protestant, let alone one who was in process of becoming a Minister. "However," she said, "I have a very nice Protestant friend who I think would be just right for you!"

She was absolutely right about that. I met Jeannie, and within six months we were married. She is my best friend and my soul mate. Without her support, I could never have accomplished the things I did since she became my wife.

My father died, and a very large piece of my life was now missing. But Jeannie helped me fill it, and after forty-five years of marriage and three children and seven wonderful grandchildren, I love her more than ever.

I was ordained a minister in the United Church of Christ in November, 1964. and was called to serve Immanuel UCC in Bromley, Kentucky. My life in the ministry, as improbable as it would have sounded just a short time before, was a reality, as Jeannie and I faced the world together.

CHAPTER VIII

A CALL FOR HELP FROM HAITI

"Behold, a man from Ethiopia …was returning and sitting in his chariot reading Esais the prophet. Then the spirit said to Philip, Go near and join thyself to this chariot"
Acts 8: 27-29 (KJV)

Since that bright day in November, 1964, when I was called to serve the little church in Bromley, Kentucky, I have preached hundreds of sermons; traveled many thousands of miles: met the most righteous saints and vilest of sinners: rejoiced with friends and families at innumerable baptisms, confirmations and weddings; suffered with them through illness and death; and grieved with them at the graveside. I suppose I should arrange these memories in some sort of order, with a set time and place to make more sense of it. But memories come to me in a disconnected way -- in chunks, some large and others small. The small chunks of disappointments are most easily forgotten, and I wonder today: "Why did I worry about that anyway?" The joys come in larger chunks, and as the old hymn says, they grow sweeter as the years go by.

I told you that I have encountered sinners along the way. I have also encountered miracles and angels. One of these "adventures" began in Cincinnati while I was the Pastor at Philippus Church in the downtown area of the city.

There is a radio station in Cincinnati with call letters, WCKY, and at that time there was a religious program running on it called the Cathedral Hour. The Cincinnati Council of Churches supported it, and at one of our meetings, it was reported that the program needed a director. Who was willing to take on the task? Since no hands were raised, I raised mine. And I accepted the job gladly, little realizing that programming for a half hour radio show is a very demanding job.

I solicited help from all the religious communities in the area and soon was doing a pretty good job of providing religious programming of an ecumenical nature, featuring ministers, of all denominations; priests and rabbis as well.

By a fluke of nature – or as I like to think of it, a miracle designed by the hand of God – the radio waves from WCKY flowed out from Ohio over the Caribbean one Sunday morning and reached a young black man in Port au Prince, Haiti. He wrote us a letter saying that he had heard our program and telling us of the great needs in his country. "What can you do to help us?" he pleaded. Very little, as it turned out.

We raised a few dollars from among some of the churches, and that was the end of it. Or so I thought. The plight of Haiti haunted me for several years to come. I knew nothing about the place. So I began reading as much as I could about this rough and mountainous little country, occupying half of the island of Hispaniola. It's only about 75 miles wide and about as long. It's not a tropical paradise as I imagined, but sits smack in the middle of the hurricane belt, and suffers accordingly.

There are over eight million people squashed together in an area smaller than Maryland, without much arable land. The people try to exist on small farms: rice, sugar cane and such. But two-thirds of the work force has no work to do. About 80% of them live below the poverty line. They have one of the highest infant mortality rates in the world.

As I learned more about Haiti, I found that it was settled by the French in the 1600's, and to this day the national language is French and Creole. The French based the economy on lumber and sugar cane, and they brought thousands of slaves from West Africa to cut down most of the trees and till the soil. Eventually these slaves revolted and established a black republic. But by the 1950s', and all the way through to the 1980's, a particularly cruel dictatorship was maintained by the Duvalier family. "Papa Doc" ruled the country and brutalized the people.

The years passed, and I found myself called to a church in Greenville, Ohio. There was a small youth group there, and I began to pray for ways to build it up. I wrote to the young man in Haiti who was now operating the Good Shepherd Orphanage in Port-au-Prince, the capital city. After all those years, he was delighted to hear from me, and together we made plans for a mission trip.

I told the kids in Greenville that if they could organize themselves and attract a few new members, we would make the journey to Haiti. A leap of faith on my part. Especially since some of my parishioners asked me why I wanted to GO to Haiti, when so many Haitians wanted so badly to LEAVE the country. They would been even more concerned if they had read one of the brochures I had seen which described Haiti as "a land of despair, and not for the light hearted tourist."

Soon we had a group of over twenty young people committed to the project. Jeannie, and I suddenly became tour arrangers with the help of AAA and began working out the logistics that would assure that the trip would be as productive, exciting, and safe as possible. Our youth group raised money with special projects, and we received encouragement and donations from members and non-members alike. Soon we found ourselves flying over the Caribbean to the exotic country of Haiti, literally on the wings of many angels.

We had no illusions about what we faced, but the reality was worse than we imagined.

As we drove from the airport to our hotel, we found ourselves in a massive traffic jam consisting of all types and sizes of buses, "ancient" cars and taxis; garishly painted and heavily overloaded trucks; goats, pigs, donkeys and dogs of every color and breed. Along the roadside, and sometimes darting into traffic, were people carrying or pushing wagons with every type of large bundle or crate imaginable. Smoke from piles of smoldering garbage mixed with exhaust fumes – and all of it made more made more noxious by the boiling heat and humidity – was almost overpowering. Besides all this, nearly every vehicle was honking its horn furiously.

We were booked into a hotel just outside the city but near the orphanage. It was seedy, to say the least. There was a swimming pool, but the water was a kind of "slime green." It was extremely hot and humid. A tarantula spider was among the strange insects that greeted us. Nevertheless, we set up shop to do whatever good works they asked us to undertake with good humor and the best intentions. We quickly found that the Haitians who worked beside us were caring and loving, always polite and ever willing to lend a hand as we clumsily handled the paint brushes and the hammers. These were good people who had been used badly. They laughed a lot, and constantly "bent over backwards" to make us feel welcome.

The work was laid out for us. A small church needed painting, and there was a need for a new room to be added to The Good Shepherd Orphanage. It was hard work, complete with lots of sweat, blisters and splinters, but we accomplished it in spite of the tropical heat and dismal conditions.

There was one very bright note that made our trip worthwhile. During our time-out periods, we made friends with the beautiful black children at the orphanage who were so eager to greet us with hugs and kisses. They were starved for affection, and they swarmed over us. When they saw us coming down the path each day toward the orphanage, they ran forward over the hard stone path, barefooted – so grateful to have someone, anyone, to spend time with them.

We organized crafts and music sessions; ball games; sports of all kinds. When it was time to leave each day, they begged us to stay just a bit longer. It was an enlightening experience for our well-fed and well-dressed kids from Ohio who had never seen scenes of poverty and deprivation. A real eye-opener. And these were children living in a comparatively safe and hygienic environment within a caring Christian community. We could only imagine the conditions of the children who lived in the streets and slums of the nearby city, where sanitation and health care did not exist.

Our only mistake was to allow some of the girls in our group to sunbathe on the roof of our hotel during an afternoon rest period. The Caribbean sun can be brutal in midday, and as a result we had several cases of bad sunburns, plus dehydration. With a lot of care, the girls revived quickly, and were none the worse for wear. Everyone of them told us that they were better for having come to Haiti. Two of them said they had decided to become nurses as a result of the trip. Many said that they hoped to return, and several of them did in the years to come.

When we retuned to Ohio, we began to tell people of what we had seen and done, and there were immediate reactions from folks who wanted to help.

I told you that it was a miracle that our message of hope had somehow moved through the radio waves from Cincinnati to the Caribbean. It was a miracle that we could persuade Ohio parents to send their children off to a country of which they knew little, and the little part they knew was discouraging to say the least.

Now I need to tell you that besides the miracle, I also encountered an angel with the name of Betsy Gump. Bessie was a middle-aged, no-nonsense type of person who attended the church I had served in Cincinnati. She heard about our mission trip and called me on the telephone one morning. "What do they need down there?" she said on the phone. I began to make a very long recital of all of the needs of the orphanage, and she cut me off. "Come down here to Cincinnati," she said, "and pick me up."

I drove to Cincinnati to talk with Betsy, and she immediately promised to supply a new refrigerator to the orphanage. We drove directly to an appliance store nearby. She picked one out, and made arrangements to have it shipped to Port-au-Prince. Just like that. Then we went to a shoe store. As she looked at a pile of of summer shoes of all sizes and shapes she asked the proprietor how much they cost. He said "$2.95". "I don't mean one pair," she said with a tone of annoyance in her voice. "How much for all of them?" He gave her a figure; she gave him a check; and soon there were many children in Haiti who received the first pair of shoes they had ever worn. From that point on, Betsy was the anonymous provider of untold amounts of money, food, and clothing that found their way from Ohio to the orphanage in Haiti. She made several trips to Haiti and about two tons of food accompanied her each time. As she once said to me: **"I have a lot of money and I have to spend it before I go."**

I realized then that there are a great many people in this world who "want to do something", but few of them know exactly how to begin to do it. This is where the church comes in. This is where Christians can make a difference by offering challenges and providing the logistics for angels such as Betsy to share their resources. It was a lesson that I was to carry with me as we implemented SARA many years in the future. While I did not have a name for it yet, I knew that I wanted to be part of a ministry where Christians can serve as a divine connection between those who are in need, and those who can fill the need. These are not the only miracles I encountered in my thirty three years as an active Pastor, nor was Betsy the only angel I met along the way. Let me tell you more.

CHAPTER IX

IMAGINE SHAKING HANDS WITH THE PRESIDENT

My cup runneth over
Psalm 23:5 (KJV)

If you want to hear about another miracle that happened to me, just think about this.

Imagine a young immigrant arriving in the United States with hardly a penny to his name or a shirt on his back, unable to speak more than a few words of English. Imagine that he has been wandering through Europe with no proper address. Consider that this young fellow is a "man without a country", inasmuch as he had to crawl through the Iron Curtain without a passport from his native Czechoslovakia. Furthermore, he considers himself a Hungarian, although the part of Hungary he lived in was part of a disputed territory which was conquered by the Russians but which now belongs to Ukraine.

Imagine further that he has little or no knowledge about the American political system, and absolutely no connections with even a city ward politician, let alone a United States Congressman or Senator. He has a "funny name" to boot, which nobody seems able to spell.

Now imagine that although not a great many years have passed since he arrived in America, this same young man, with his family beside him, is shaking the hand of the President of the United States and delivering a sermon to him and his family on Mother's Day, 1970.

This is the kind of a miracle that can only happen in a country like the United States. I tell you honestly that only an immigrant like me can truly appreciate what we have going for us in this country. Many Americans are unaware that in many of the communist countries where I lived, as well as in totalitarian countries around the world today, the heads of state are not open and accessible and certainly not cordial with the people living there. In fact, they separate themselves from their own government officials and political cronies for fear that they will be replaced or assassinated. They create barriers for the common people that keep them "in", and they make it difficult to send help from abroad. We found this out when we began to assist people in Eastern Europe with SARA.

I am very proud to be an American, if only as an adopted son, and I am a patriot without shame. I have continuing faith in American ideals, and I am deeply grateful that our country is a staunch protector of personal freedom. I pride myself that in addition to preaching, I also find time to lecture wherever and whenever I can on the theme: "What's Right with America."

This is why my visit with President Nixon in 1970 has been a highlight of my life, and a joy forever.

It all began while I was preaching at Philippus Church in Cincinnati. This large and impressive church sits at the end of Race Street in the "over-the-Rhine" district of the city. The steeple can be seen all the way from downtown….after all, it has a six foot tall golden Finger pointing toward Heaven.

When I became Pastor at Philippus I noticed a leaden plate covering the rose window half way up the steeple. This was at the height of the Vietnam War, so I proposed to the church council that we uncover the rose window, and add a symbolic cross over a helmet as a tribute to our soldiers fighting and dying in Vietnam. And in October, 1968, we did just that. It was perhaps the first unofficial memorial to Vietnam Vets. It still stays lit at night as a radiant beacon for the city.

We had the honor of the presence of Senator William Saxbe at the dedication. I contacted Wright Patterson Air Force Base in Dayton, hoping that they might provide a color guard. They responded with a forty piece military band! It was an impressive and memorable occasion to say the least.

In ways I still do not completely understand, my name circulated among various political entities in the next two years. At any rate, the telephone rang in our home on the morning of Monday, May 4, 1970, just as I was scurrying out the door for a funeral. I had told Jeannie to tell anyone who was calling that I was not at home. When she answered, the person on the other end of the line said: "This is the White House calling. Is Reverend Szilagyi there?"

Of course, I ran back immediately and was greeted by the voice of Ms Lucille Winchester, President Nixon's social secretary. She indicated that President and Mrs. Nixon would be honored if I would accept an invitation to preach the Mother's Day sermon on the following Sunday in the White House. I choked away tears when I told her that I would be much more honored than they.

We were living very close to the poverty line at that time, with two small children and a baby in arms. The clothes I wore were purchased at rummage sales, or were gifts from the widows of church members who I buried. I knew I had to have something suitable for a meeting with the President. So I made a deal with a member who was the manager of a men's clothing store. I promised him that if he gave me a suit, I would manage to get a photograph of me and the suit standing next to the President. He very willingly gave me one, and it was a beautiful suit that I wore with pride for many years to come.

When Jean and I and our three children landed at the airport in Washington, a man in a black suit came up to me and said: "Rev. Szilagyi, I am here to take you to the Manger Hay Adams" -- a very fine hotel indeed. As we settled into our rooms, I stood on the balcony facing the White House and watched a large crowd of demonstrators creating a disturbance in the square in front of it. The President had sent troops into Cambodia just days before, and the streets were full of people. Some were honest demonstrators. Others were just very intoxicated and disorderly.

I decided to go downstairs into the streets and talk with some of them. I sympathized with those who were sincere in their cause, but I was shocked at the hatred and confusion many of these kids had about our political system. Obviously, they could not visualize the fear which my family experienced in Czechoslovakia whenever we heard a knock on the door at night….or the dread which the Jews felt as they were trucked to Auschwitz…or the foreboding that the citizens of Budapest felt when they realized that "the Russians were coming"….or the horror that the Haitians experienced when Papa Doc's goon squads raided their village. And so it goes on and on to this day throughout Afghanistan and Iraq and Gaza. How lucky our young people are to be living where they live!

My daughter, Nathalie, and baby Mike, were too young to accompany us to the White House. George, who was seven, just managed to meet qualifications, but Nathalie complained that she should have been the one to go, because she behaved better than her older brother. Which was altogether true.

A large, black limousine picked us up at the hotel on Sunday morning, and drove us up to the front gate at the south entrance to the White House. When we arrived at the gate, the guard asked our name, and I spelled it out: S-Z-I-L-A-G-Y-I...

He came back in a few moments and said: "There's no one on this list by that name." I thought to myself that I knew it was too good to be true. Jean was ready for tears as she clutched George's hand. Then the guard looked down once again at the list and said: "I'm so sorry. You are the speaker today, the **FIRST** name on the list." With great relief we were admitted to the White House.

We brought some small gifts: a package of letters from George's school friends, and of course some "keszimunka" which is a traditional type of Hungarian embroidered linen. There was lots of pomp and brass, and all very exciting.

We were escorted into the Nixon family living room, and soon the President reached his hand out to us. I declined his offer of coffee and sweet rolls and told him I would rather talk with him and offer my support for our country's involvement to keep people free in a country faced by communism. After all, I was a living example of what could happen to good people attempting to survive under a bad system. Jean had great empathy for Mrs. Nixon, who remained very warm and cordial, despite the fact that she had to listen day in and day out to alleged atrocities being committed by her husband in Asia.

After a while, Julie and David Eisenhower and Tricia joined us. What a wonderful feeling to descend the staircase and enter the East Room.

At one point, the President stopped and said: "This is the point where the band starts to play the national anthems of all visitors who are heads of state, and there are quite a few of them here today." He smiled at me: "Today you are part of American history."

The choir that morning, recommended by Senator Gerald Ford, was from Calvin College, and they sang a beautiful old anthem: "Precious Lord, Take my Hand." I certainly felt that Jesus was leading me on this special day in my life through this very grand and important crowd which had gathered for Mother's Day service. My sermon seemed to be well-received.

At the close of the service as we left the room, I recognized a dignified woman on one side of the room. The late Senator Everett Dirksen of Illinois was one of my favorite speakers, and when I recognized his wife standing there, I politely asked the President if he would mind if I broke protocol and give her a hug. He answered with a laugh: "Of course!" I told Mrs Dirksen how much I admired her husband's wit and his wonderful voice, and how every great man had a great woman standing behind him. The President motioned to one of his aides and asked him to send me some of the Senator's recordings. I received them shortly after we arrived home and have treasured them ever since.

When we stepped off the plane in Ohio, there were at least three television cameras and many flashing lights awaiting our reaction to the President, the worship service, and of course his comments about Cambodia. All three of the kids were tired, hungry, and screaming at this point. We made the 11:00 o'clock news. Just me. They cut out the screaming kids and the frazzled wife.

As for the sermon, an editor from Reader's Digest called me and asked for exclusive rights. It was subsequently published in a book called: "White House Sermons", together with sermons by Dr Norman Vincent Peale and Billy Graham, among others.

How did I find myself giving a sermon to the President and his family in the White House? I can scarcely believe that a naturalized citizen with a funny name and only six years into his ministry –someone with little skill in terms of writing or spelling—could have been given this opportunity. But there is no question in my mind that a person's fate is directly related to his response to Jesus Christ. When you allow Christ the first place in your life and then say: "I can do it!" you can achieve anything. I am living proof of it.

And I believe that while Christ often raises us to high ground and allows us an occasional glimpse into the pomp and circumstance of those in high office, He expects us to return as soon as possible to the needs of His people, and admonishes us to:"Feed my sheep." And occasionally He opens our eyes to miracles to reassure us that He is still very much in charge.

CHAPTER X

WHEN YOU DOUBT THAT GOD CAN PROVIDE MIRACLES, SOMETIMES HE DOUBLES HIS EFFORTS!

Mark 10: 52 And Jesus said unto him, Go thy way; thy faith hath made you whole. (KJV)

While I was preaching in a little congregation in Millvale, PA, God showed his face to one of our church families, not once, but twice…as if to make the point that miracles can still happen in this modern day and age.

There was a lovely Christian woman named Beverly in my congregation who had a son about eight years old, and was expecting another child in a few months. One evening I received a frantic telephone call from Bev telling me that her husband, Bob, had suffered a stroke. It happened while he was coaching a Little League Game. He was only thirty-eight years old, healthy and active at one moment, and in the next, flat on his back in an ambulance transporting him to the intensive care unit of a Pittsburgh Hospital. His blood pressure had soared past the 300 mark, and he soon passed into a total coma.

I immediately drove to the hospital to comfort her, and, after I saw Bob lying there unresponsive and totally motionless, I prepared her for the worst. He continued in a coma for weeks which stretched into months. In my daily visit to the IC unit, Bev and I prayed together, and waited. And waited. Bob remained at the edge of death.

Her time had come, and in a different hospital across town, she gave birth to a lovely little girl at 10:00 pm one evening. I asked one of the other "expectant fathers" who was with me in the waiting room to take a couple of Polaroid shots of the new baby, which he gladly did after I explained the situation.

We gave one of the pictures to Bev and then I rushed across town to Bob's bedside where the nurses and I called out to him: "Bob, Bob, you have a daughter, Bob. Wake up. Wake Up." He did not respond. A few days previous to this, he had been operated on for a golf-ball sized blood clot on his brain. It was doubtful that he would ever regain consciousness, and even if he did…

After many months, however, he opened his eyes one day and began to show small signs of recognition. If you would ask: "Bob, how are you?" you could almost see wheels spinning in his brain as he attempted to reply. Eventually he reached the point where he could say two words together, but only after a great deal of thought and struggle. The words were: "I'm alright."

They sent Bob to a rehabilitation center in Pittsburgh where he spent nearly a year learning how to walk again, and regain some of his speech and memory. Meanwhile, Bev struggled to take care of her little boy as well as her infant daughter. Finally, Bob was up and around, and determined to get back to work at the funeral home where he had been employed. But it just wasn't happening. When someone spoke to him, there was a ten second hesitation before he could answer. And even then, his answers were sometimes vague and incomplete.

As a special treat to celebrate their anniversary one evening, Bev took Bob to a nearby restaurant. Once again I received a frantic call from her. The unbelievable had happened! Bob had choked on a piece of steak…stopped breathing…turned blue…totally unconscious.

From that point on, a small series of miracles followed one after another. At this period in time, there was no "911 Emergency Access." Luckily, the restaurant was close by to a fire house with a medical team on hand. After a quick analysis of the situation, a call was made, and soon a helicopter was swiftly life-flighting Bob to his neurologist at a Pittsburgh hospital.

Bev was left at the restaurant and frantically trying to call me, but she could not remember how to spell my name. By another small miracle, one of the bus boys at the hotel knew our son, George, and quickly looked up our name in the phone book I was able to reach the hospital quickly from our home, and was soon on the way to the hospital with Bev.

The doctor who met us was very grim. He told us that Bob was once again in a coma, and that he wasn't sure whether he would come out of it this time. Relatives came by, and we all sat in the emergency room until 2:00am in the morning. The doctor said that there was not much use of our staying there any longer, and that he would call if the situation changed. We prayed together, asking God to be kind to this good man and his family who had suffered through so much for so long. Then we went home.

At 7:45 in the morning, I received a call from Bev. She said that she had been restless from the time she finally went to bed after she arrived home. She said that at 4:00am – and she knew it was exactly 4:00am because she looked at the clock next to her bed – she picked up the Bible and tried to read. "I don't know what I read," she said, "but I know that I started to sob. 'Lord Jesus', I said, ' I'll put Bob in your hands, and if it's your will, you can take him. But I would like to have him back, and I just can't cope anymore."

"With that", she said, "I fell asleep. And at 7:30 this morning," she continued, "the doctor called and told me that Bob had come out of his coma at exactly 4:00am that morning."

When I went to see him, he was not in his room. I yelled out: "Hey Bob, where are you?"

"I'm in the bathroom," he said. "I'll be right out." All of this in a clear strong voice. He came out and said: "Well, I don't understand what happened, but I feel perfectly alright, and I would like to go home and be with my family." I said: "Bob, do you notice the way you're talking?" He said: "Not only I notice, but everyone notices it. Now I want to get out of here, but the doctor says he wants to keep me just a bit longer so he can observe me." Bob did go home. And a short time later he went back to work at the funeral home where he had been employed many months before.

Now I want to tell you something about how God's goodness and grace works itself out among believers. The man who ran the funeral home was a very kind Jewish gentleman who continued to pay Bob's wages during all the months he spent in the hospital and the rehab center. In the years which followed, this wonderful man died suddenly of a heart attack and left his twenty-year old son to inherit the business. With Bob's help and training, the son has gone on to assume ownership and management of his father's business. The debt of kindness has been paid in full. The Bible tells us about casting our bread upon the waters. The goodness we send out always comes back many times over. And miracles do happen – sometimes twice in a row.

All of this happened about a quarter of a century ago, and I am happy to tell you that the little girl who was born at 10:00pm in the evening is going to be married next year. Her father, the man in the coma, will be present to "give her away."

God is good.

CHAPTER XI

GOD HAS A SENSE OF HUMOR

"For the Lord taketh pleasure in his people"
Psalm 149: 4 (KJV)

Bev's and Bob's story is a beautiful one, and since it contains mention of a Jewish gentlemen who did righteous deeds, I must tell you of another who I met while serving a small church in Pennsylvania

There was a man named Stan who operated a drug store which was very popular with both young and old. Stan's father and uncle founded the store in the early 20's and the family played a prominent role in all of the community's cultural events and philanthropic ventures.

When I accepted a call to this church, I soon realized that the town was about 75% per cent Roman Catholic with the remaining 25% scattered about in five small Protestant congregations. There was a very small minion of Jewish businessmen in the town, including Stan -- all of whom were notable for their good works.

I asked a member of the church consistory if he knew Stan and he immediately told me that EVERYONE knew Stan. As a new Pastor in town, I was anxious to meet him, and it was quickly arranged.

I told Stan that I was anxious to do something to recognize our church's appreciation for all the good things accomplished over the years by the Borough's small Jewish business community. I did not intend to make this a highly publicized event, but perhaps our little congregation could quietly make some sort of gesture that would help to "even the score." I explained that for one thing, we were holding a Holocaust Sunday in our church later in the year, and that we had invited the Rabbi from a very large Jewish congregation in the university district of Pittsburgh as our speaker. He accepted, and we planned to make a small contribution to a Zionist organization in the city which was buying trees to reforest Israel which, after all, was our holy land as well as their's.

Stan smiled and said he thought that would be a very nice gesture, and that he could connect us with the appropriate persons to make it happen. Then he said straight out: "There are religious Jews and secular Jews. I fall into the latter category. But I am a Jew," he said proudly. And then, as if sensing the next question he asked: "The trees are a fine idea. What would you expect in return?"

I told him that for a long time, I had wanted some water from the River Jordan with which to baptize our church babies, and I asked him if he could arrange that as well. He said he would make some inquiries.

My friend on the Church Council who had accompanied me and introduced me to Stan telephoned me later that evening.

"As soon as I arrived home," he said, "Stan called me. He said that he was not familiar with all of the Christian denominations but he knew there were different ways to baptize people in different churches. He asked whether in our church we sprinkled our members or dunked them in altogether?"

We both began to laugh because we realized that Stan was trying as diplomatically as possible to figure out whether he needed to supply just a pint or so of Jordan River water, or a whole tank car load full. I stopped in his office the next day and explained that we "sprinkled" in our church. He seemed greatly relieved so far as the logistics of the project were concerned. As you can see, even God has a sense of humor.

Within a short time, we received a quart of Jordan River water, already purified for us. We mixed it with a gallon of distilled water, and many a child has since been received into First UCC, Millvale with a sprinkling of this gift of water… and love.

Let me tell you a bit more. Shortly before we served the church in the early 1980's, a flood paralyzed the business district. Many businesses in this little mill town decided to close their doors. But Stan's store was the first to clean up and re-open, giving a clear response to whether the business district could survive. I have since learned that in September 2004 another flood—fueled by the remnants of Hurricane Ivan—and much more destructive than any ever inflicted on the community -- left the town once more in shambles. At this point, nearly a quarter of the town's businesses closed their doors forever.

And once again Stan's company, now operated by his daughter, renewed its commitment to its employees and to the community. To give you an idea of the devastation, the church which I served suffered a quarter of a million dollars damage. I'm happy to say that those good people also renewed their commitment to reconstruct and reopen. Both these institutions are anchors, in their own way, to the community, and I am proud to say that I served there, and that I knew Stan.

CHAPTER XII

THE BOY WITH THE CROOKED BACK

*"Whosoever shall receive this child
in my name, receiveth me."*
Luke 9:48 (KJV)

It was a great joy, indeed a blessing, for Jean and I to visit Hungary again in the summer of 1988. I didn't realize how great a blessing it was to be until we were ready to leave for home. In a set of circumstances which could only have been planned by God, we encountered a little boy with a crooked back just before we left.

I organized the trip to acquaint the young people in my congregation in Cleveland with their Hungarian heritage. I was Pastor of the First Hungarian Reformed Church on Buckeye Road at the time.

At one time, this church had several thousand members. The building was absolutely beautiful, constructed in the form of a Cathedral. Architectural students from local colleges and universities often stopped by to study the features of the structure and the steeple, particularly, which rose over 160 feet in the air. Once, the steeple overlooked a large and thriving Hungarian congregation, but now there were far less. The movement to the suburbs carried away most of them.

As a means of reviving interest and instilling pride of heritage in the three or four hundred who still remained, and who came long distances to worship, I organized a trip to Hungary which included all the places of interest which I thought they should see. Eighty-six people participated in the trip, including myself and wife Jeannie. We were particularly anxious to see our oldest son, George, who was a dental student in the city of Pecs.

The Youth Group of our church raised money with various "good works", and even organized a small dance group which performed at various places as we toured Hungary. Everyone had an exciting and rewarding experience. And now it was time to go home.

While the rest of the tour party left for Cleveland, Jean and I stayed behind for just a few more days of visiting with George. That was a blessing in itself, but more was to come. We had eaten heartily of the wonderful Magyar cuisine: lots of fried chicken, pork cutlets, dumplings, sour cream and paprika. Lots and lots of paprika. Perhaps a bit too hearty for Jeannie who had a queasy stomach even before we stopped for lunch at a restaurant in a small town near Pecs. The restaurant did not offer "wonderful Magyar cuisine"but instead featured pizza, of all things, with an assortment of ingredients which included very hot and pungent Hungarian sausage accompanied by a bottle of ketchup.

It was a steamy hot day in mid-summer, and the windows of the restaurant were open. There was an outdoor toilet facility nearby, and a host of insects that zoomed here and there. Need I say more. Jeannie was very uncomfortable, and becoming moreso every minute.

We started our drive back to Pecs, and about fifteen minutes later, Jeannie put her hand up and said, grimly: "Hurry up and find a bathroom!" We stopped at the only place which was open in a small village: a crossroads café where all the locals hung out. But very welcome to Jeannie at that point.

As George and I waited at the car, I saw three boys standing across the street. Two of them were sturdy fellows leaning against their bicycles. The third was a very short lad with a large hump on his back, standing very crookedly between the two other boys with straight, strong backs. Because I have been blessed with three healthy children, I always say a prayer when I see a child who is not. My prayer that day was: "I wish I could help that kid, but I just don't have that kind of money, and besides, I don't know anybody I can turn to who would help me with this."

I made the typical excuses that we all do in life when confronted with a challenge to help someone: "That's not my job"; "I am not able to do it"; "It's not my responsibility"; "Let someone else do it"; "Let the government do it."

By now my wife had returned, and we left. But as we traveled down the road toward Pecs, I could not stop thinking about the boy with the crooked back, and how I was leaving him to his fate. But not for very long, because Jean said very suddenly and very painfully: "Turn around and go back. Hurry. Hurry. Hurry!"

We returned to the same seedy café, and once again I was standing outside the car. The boy with the crooked back was still standing on the corner. I suppose the other two boys had already left on their bicycles for an afternoon of fun. I began to talk to God once more: "Lord," I said, "You don't have to hit me over the head to let me know that you want me to do something for this child. Show me how, Lord, and help me do it, and I WILL do it."

George lived about half an hour from that little crossroads and promised me that he would go back to the village and hunt until he found him. I promised him that if he could find the boy, I would find help for him.

How could I not feel compassion for that child, since I knew that physically deformed children in rural Europe, and especially eastern Europe, suffer a double stigma. They are crippled in body and in mind, because they are often regarded as curiosities and freaks. I was horrified by thoughts of deformed and disabled children arriving in Auschwitz from my own home town, and being herded into the gas chambers as Mr Kovar had described it to me in Atlantic City. This boy was not a freak in the eyes of God, and certainly not in the eyes of this American. I knew something must be done…if only for one little boy.

Jean was feeling much better, and we left once again for Pecs, leaving the boy on the corner.

On the following evening, we went to dinner with an official from George's medical school. I asked if anything could be done for a boy with a crooked back such as the one who we had seen. He explained that the child was probably suffering from scoliosis. It is quite common in eastern Europe, where hundreds – perhaps thousands of little children are doomed to short, painful lives with deformed backs. He explained some of the medical procedures which are necessary, but not performed in Pecs or in all of Hungary for that matter, because of the lack of fully trained specialists and the necessary equipment.

Of course, Jeannie and I were aware of what needed to be done for the child, but not how to provide the means to do it.

And so we returned to Cleveland, but a thought was already developing in my mind. God does not let prayers go unanswered. When you ask Him to "show me", he does.

CHAPTER XIII

THE ANSWER WAS AT MY FINGER TIPS

"Seek and ye shall find" Luke 11:9 (KJV)

The first day Jean and I were back in Cleveland, I telephoned a fellow by the name of Bob Zigaric who was connected with the Shrine Temple in Cleveland. I told him about the little boy with the crooked back who we encountered in Hungary, and asked Bob if something could be done. He immediately said to me: "Come on over and we'll talk about it."

God's answer to my prayer, I found to my surprise, was at my fingertips, just a telephone call away.

The Shriners are best known for their funny hats, their turned-up shoes, and the tiny cars which they drive in parades. But while they have a great deal of fun, they also do good works. Lots of good works. They manage a network of Hospitals for Crippled Children and Burn Patients throughout the country, and any child who needs hospital care receives it without charge and without respect to race, religion, or nationality.

If a child has health insurance, they will accept it. But if, for instance, the operation costs $100,000 and the insurance only pays $10, it is enough. If a child needs more specialized care, they will even pay for the expense at another hospital. It is probably one of the largest and most unselfish private philanthropic operations of its kind in the world.

I went to see Bob the following morning. He said "yes", they can do the specialized operation and the rehabilitation involved with scoliosis. He would need x-rays of the child, of course, and a full medical diagnosis. He felt that something could be done for the boy, and told me that the nearest Shrine Hospital was in Erie, PA, about twenty miles away from our new home in Conneaut, Ohio.

I immediately telephoned my son, George, in Hungary, and told him to find the boy and tell his parents that there was an opportunity to help him. I knew it might be a difficult task because in that part of Europe, parents often hide a child away who is physically deformed. And as we know, in Hitler's time these children were simply and swiftly exterminated.

George wasted no time in contacting officials at the medical school and staff members of the local children's clinic.

Some of those at the clinic remembered a little boy who resembled George's description. Apparently he had problems other than scoliosis and had been operated on for a club foot some years before. After some strenuous searching, little Miklos was found.

God's hand had already intervened. His mother told us later that just two weeks before we arrived with our tour group, she had read an article in which a child with the same deformity had been described. She told us that after she read it, she fell to her knees and prayed: "Why can't my son be helped? Please help him, Lord."

A member of my congregation, John Pustai, took it upon himself to find enough money to provide a round-trip ticket from Hungary to Cleveland for Miklos. Remember that Hungary was still a communist country at that point. People did not easily cross borders and simply come and go as they pleased. Officially, Hungary was not a Christian country and might not respond to a Protestant minister like myself. In the course of events since the communist takeover after World War II, the government had not dealt gently with priests or pastors. They had even gone so far as to imprison a Cardinal of the Catholic Church.

In addition to that potential roadblock, the hospital required that a parent who could sign permission slips for the surgery must accompany the child. Once again, John Pustai worked with some of his friends in the Shrine and came up with two tickets: one for Miklos and another for his father.

Now, somehow, we had to penetrate the Iron Curtain to bring them to Cleveland. We turned to the Hungarian Embassy in Washington, fully expecting some obstructions and objections in dealing with a matter of this kind. The problems of a little boy did, indeed, seem insignificant when viewed with the affairs of state. Somehow, I managed to speak with the First Secretary himself at the Embassy. He was moved by our story. So moved that this dedicated communist said to me: "May God bless you. You have shown such compassion for this Hungarian child that we will do everything in our power to make sure that Budapest understands the situation and acts on it promptly." And apparently, that is exactly what he did. Permission was granted and visas issued.

There was just one more obstacle to overcome, and that was action by the Board of Directors of the Children's Hospital to accept a foreign child. Once again we expected the Board to take considerable time in making a decision which involved a very poor little boy without medical insurance of any kind coming to them for an expensive operation from a communist country.

Dr. Frankovich, Chief of Staff at the hospital quickly cut through the red tape and allayed our fears. "I have reviewed the x-rays", he said, "and I think we can help this child. You may assume that little Miklos will be operated on here." As simple and wonderful as that.

The family in Hungary was notified, and Miklos and his father were soon jetting over the Atlantic, bound for Cleveland. We later learned that his family were not Hungarians at all, but Croatians living in Hungary. Moreover, they were Roman Catholics. But what did that matter? God had seen a need and somehow placed me in the flow of coincidences which solved the problem.

After getting Dr. Frankovitch's analysis and authorization for the operation that day in August, 1988, I walked from his office to my car and cried a little and prayed a lot, thanking God for the opportunity to help this child. This was the moment that the ministry that was soon to be known as SARA was conceived. And SARA was to consume my life from that moment on.

CHAPTER XIV

MIKLOS ARRIVES

"I was a stranger, and ye took me in." Matthew 25:35 (KJV)

A frightened little boy stepped off an airplane in Cleveland, facing a crowd of about fifty well-wishers, in addition to newspaper people and a camera man from the local TV station.

Miklos immediately began to cry: "They are all looking at me, the way I am!"

He was so used to being abused and stared at in his village that he could not comprehend that complete strangers were willing to share their love, their prayers and their resources to help him walk straight. But it was not an easy road for him, or for us. And it would take time for his surgery to be scheduled and performed.

First, we felt that he should learn to speak English so that he could communicate better with the doctors who were going to help him. A wonderful teacher named Audrey Punkar agreed to tutor him, and soon had him chatting away in his new tongue. Friends from the neighboring Baptist Church came by with clothes and toys.

A kind Hungarian gentleman in Erie offered Miklos' father a job. This was not as easy as it seems. Because he was an alien, permission had to be granted for the authorization of a temporary work permit. Our good Shriners contacted Pennsylvania Congressman

Ridge, who later became Governor of the Commonwealth and later the Director of Homeland Security. He immediately took the project under his wing and permission was granted.

In the meantime, I decided that since Miklos and his father were Roman Catholics, they should be introduced to the Catholic community and encouraged to attend a Catholic church in the area. I called the Knights of Columbus who arranged a meeting between the boy and his father and Bishop Malone. The Knights agreed to pick the two of them up each Sunday morning and deliver them to mass. We were all of one mind in agreeing that a child in need is, well, a child in need, no matter what his religion, race or nationality is.

This is what is so great about being an American and recognizing that compassion without strings attached is one of our nation's greatest strengths. As one of the members of my congregation put it: **"We are just so glad that Miklos is here, and that we are able to help him."**

When it came time for the operation, it was decided that he should be sent to the Shriners Hospital in Chicago where a noted specialist, Dr. Lubyki, would perform the delicate operation…or, as it turned out…two separate six-hour long operations. Miklos' physical condition had caused problems with his rib cage and chest cavity. For another thing, one leg was several inches shorter than the other. All of this entailed extensive surgery. The doctors agreed that in his pre-operative condition, Miklos could not have expected to live beyond the age of twenty.

The operations were performed, with extensive hospital stays and considerable pain for the boy. Then rehabilitation began, and it was a long and painful ordeal for the child. He was sent back to the hospital in Erie where a doctor specialized in stretching leg bones. A metal contraption was affixed to his right foot which pulled on the bone. The foot had to be pulled, then cut, then healed. Then the process began again: pull, cut and heal. And again. This went on for a long time, and was very painful for an adult, much less a small child in a strange country.

Miklos had to overcome several infections in the process. And all the while, of course, he was homesick for his mother and his friends. He wanted to go back home. He was, after all, a brave little boy, but just a little boy.

To make his ordeal a bit more bearable, a number of people in the community began to raise money to bring his mother to his side. The Knights of Columbus held a spaghetti dinner; other groups conducted bake sales and other money-making projects. A newspaper woman named Diana Lewis began writing articles in the paper about the child and his ordeal, and she added the fact that an apartment was needed so that the family could be re-united.

God sent an angel in the form of a man named Jim Fedor who quickly donated a furnished a furnished apartment for the duration of their stay. He simply told me: "They can have it for free." Moreover, he paid the utilities and even put food in the refrigerator. Through his kindness, the family was reunited under their own roof, gaining a sense of security and dignity after a long separation. Surely that mother must have marveled at how her short, desperate prayer many months before had unleashed a deluge of goodwill from total strangers in a strange land.

The miracle is that nine out of ten Americans are willing to take to heart those in need, and to share their love and resources unselfishly. They simply need someone to "nudge" them. And I was more than happy to do that, because I, too, had experienced being a stranger in a strange land many years before.

A year and a half had now passed since little Miklos had arrived in Cleveland and shuffled down the steps of the plane with a large hump on his back. Now, as he prepared to board the plane for home, he literally ran up the steps. Jean and I hugged each other as the plane took off. "He's walking tall", I said.

America has so much to offer in terms of medical knowledge and resources. Somehow we had to manage to share America's resources abroad. Somehow we had to continue nudging people to do the right thing, knowing that once they do it, they will continue to do it, again and again. As we walked through the airport to our car, Jean said to me: "What now?" And once again, God intervened with a simple answer to what seemed to be an insurmountable problem.

CHAPTER XV

SARA IS BORN

Genesis 18:13 "And the Lord said unto Abraham, wherefore did Sarah laugh saying, shall I of a surety bear a child... Is anything too hard for the Lord?" (KJV)

Jean and I rejoiced as we walked from the airport toward the parking lot after putting Miklos on the plane. He had come to us as a frightened child with a crooked back and no hope for the future. He returned home a young man, standing straight, and confident in his future. We rejoiced, but then came to the same somber conclusion.

Even if we managed to bring one child with scoliosis to the United States each year, we would make only a tiny dent in the total picture. Perhaps 12-15 children would be fortunate enough in the next decade to come and be cured. But there were thousands who would never receive the chance to walk straight.

But -- and it was a big BUT -- what if we could bring doctors from over there, in Hungary, to America where they could be trained in the specialized medical techniques that would cure scoliosis and straightens little backs. The doctors could, in turn, return to Hungary and cure hundreds, perhaps thousands, throughout their careers.

There was a very kind gentleman named Dick Brzuz who was administrator of the Shriners Hospital in Erie. We went to see him. And we asked: "Can this be done? And can you help us do it?"

Considering that we were living on a preacher's salary and that all of our funds would have to be voluntary, it seemed an impossible question:

"Can this be done?"

Dick talked with his national headquarters, and the answer came back as a positive. "If you can provide the surgeon, we will do the rest." Immediately I contacted our son, George, a Student Dentist in Pecs, Hungary, who had many contacts in the medical clinic there. They suggested a young man named Arpad Bellyei who was an orthopedic surgeon slated to become Head of the University Medical School in Pecs. He immediately agreed, and thanks to the good Shriners, was soon on his way to Ohio.

During his residency, Arpad stayed in our home, studying in his room for hours on end, going through books, watching tapes. He was an extremely intelligent and very skilled orthopedic surgeon, and soon he had acquired the skills which would allow him to carry his knowledge back to Hungary where, in time, many hundreds of children could be "made straight."

Before he returned home to Hungary he said to me: "Steve, my budget for new equipment at the Medical School in Pecs is about $9,000 a year in terms of US dollars. The cost of *just three or four medical rods* to straighten a child's back is over $10,000. I have learned a wonderful procedure, but with limited resources I could only do perhaps two or three operations a year. I need help. What can you do?"

I contacted a friend, State Senator Boggs of Ohio, who in turn got in touch with Dr Ronald Fletcher who was the Director of

Health for the State of Ohio. There have been many angels in my life who intervened at critical junctures and Dr Fletcher was certainly one of them. Arpad and I sat across from him at lunch at the Holiday Inn in Youngstown and we presented our case for the medical problems in Hungary and the need for orthopedic medical equipment. After he heard us out, he smiled at Arpad and said: "Shall we help just your hospital or the whole country?" I leaned over and impulsively kissed Fletcher on his bearded cheek.

"God bless you" I said. "We asked for a little and you want to give us much more than we dreamed of."

Dr Fletcher arranged for Arpad to meet Governor Celeste, and initiated an assistance program for the Medical School in Pecs. Dr. Edward Kilroy, a stately and very compassionate man slightly older than me, was scheduled to move into Fletcher's position very shortly. So I arranged to meet him. He felt a bit uncomfortable with me at first. He was a staunch Roman Catholic and didn't know whether to address me as "Father", "Reverend" or simply "Mister."

"Look," I said, "We are both professional people, and you are not that much older than I am. So you can call me Steve, and I'll call you Ed." That broke the ice and he immediately agreed to carry on what Dr Fletcher had promised. He appointed Dr Gary Crumb to take charge of what was to become the SARA project, and now both the Governor's Office as well as the Ohio Hospital Association got involved. As a result, about $15,000,000 worth of medical supplies --roughly twenty-four ship containers—were on their way to Hungary.

How quickly the word spread. One evening the Hungarian Ambassador to the United States telephoned me at home and said: "My wife recently met President Bush's wife, and she told her that she had seen something while on a trip to Hungary with the

President that upset her very much." She explained that it was the sight of many, many children who were blinded at birth because of inadequacies of incubators, or lack of them, in Hungarian hospitals. There was often a lack of oxygen, or too much oxygen, in the incubators.

"Can you do something about that?" asked the Ambassador.

I could, and I did by contacting Dr. Anthony at University Hospitals in Cleveland. Soon a shipment of modern incubators with his name tag on them were on their way to Hungary. We gave our message to the folks at the Cleveland Clinic, and immediately we were receiving gifts from various departments in the Clinic: orthopedic instruments from the Bone and Muscle Research Department; all kinds of equipment. Everybody down the line gave us gifts of one kind or another to send overseas, and all of them useful and much needed.

The appeals for help began to come from all quarters. I received a message from the Reformed Bishop of Budapest who asked that we remember his people in parts of Rumania and Ukraine which used to be Hungarian territories many years earlier. The needs were growing well beyond our resources and our knowledge of the situation. So I formed a committee of interested people who could visit eastern Europe and see for ourselves where there were the most immediate medical crises. Carl Eldred, Martha Tomlinson, and Dr Vita Draulis quickly agreed to participate. Dr Draulis spoke Russian fluently and understood conditions behind the Iron Curtain.

We had good intentions, but no money, so I turned to the President of the Ohio Conference, United Church of Christ, who sent us over $3000 toward transportation. In the years ahead when we were organized as a non-profit, ecumenical ministry it was in affiliation with the United Church of Christ. The UCC has been the anchor of our ministry from that time on, and our partnership has been fruitful and rewarding. More about that will be forthcoming in chapters to come.

We were soon on our way to eastern Europe. Our little group began its tour in Hungary where we visited a number of hospitals which were, to say the least, deplorable. The Women's Hospital in particular was a disgrace. Totally unsanitary. Very, very bad. The needs were overwhelming. From there we went to Ukraine and then on to Romania. In Romania we found a Reformed Bishop who had international contacts and was very willing to participate with us in getting medical help of the kind which we were proposing.

Our little committee all agreed that the need was greatest in Ukraine. There, the medical needs went far beyond scoliosis. In Ukraine, for example, it was brought to our attention that practically no one owned a pair of glasses. Before we left, we contacted an optometrist by the name of Bill Campbell who was the president of the Volunteer Optometric Service to Humanity in Ohio.

As a result, over 25,000 pairs of glasses were soon on their way to Ukraine. We arranged to set up two facilities near the border where recipients could be examined and then fitted with the appropriate lenses on the spot. We learned later that Ukrainians lined up for a quarter of a mile to receive them. From that time on, thousands more pairs of glasses were sent over, providing the gift of sight without respect to politics, religion, or nationality.

When we returned to Ohio, we took a reality check. We realized that the work was expanding faster than we could have ever anticipated, and that we needed to incorporate our little group. We also realized that we needed something on paper that people who contributed could recognize. When we completed the legal work, the question arose: "So what were we going to call this new child of ours?"

It happened that our first grandchild was named Sara. Using her initials, we suddenly received an epiphany: a "bolt from the blue" Why not use the initials S.A.R.A. to read: "Sharing America's Resources Abroad." Because that is exactly what we were urging Americans to do.

So SARA was born and Christened with an appropriate name. Now she needed Godparents! Perhaps the new UCC Ohio Conference Minister might agree to sponsor "our child."

CHAPTER XVI

SARA NEEDED GODPARENTS, SO WE DISCUSSED IT OVER A PLATE OF "PAPRIKAS CSIKE"

Luke 2:22 When the days of her purification....were accomplished, they brought him to Jerusalem to present him to the Lord (KJV)

As I told you, our ministry of sharing America's resources abroad began by helping one child and by training one physician. It was a small beginning, but rapidly expanding with a growing need for financial support. The ministry now had a name -- SARA -- but it needed structure and sponsors, or in the words of the church, "some worthy godparents." We looked toward the UCC Conference Office in Columbus for inspiration, inasmuch as The Reverend Thomas Dipko who was serving as Conference Minister at that time was one of our earliest supporters.

By now, a man from New Bremen, Ohio – Dr Ralph Quellhorst – had recently assumed the post of Conference Minister for the Ohio Conference of the UCC. As I got to know Ralph through telephone calls and correspondence, I described some of the projects in which SARA was participating. He expressed an immediate and genuine interest.

I explained that all of our work is done on a volunteer basis, but at the very least we need financial assistance to help pay for transportation costs of medical equipment and supplies so graciously and freely contributed. I told him that the denominational offices, based in New York City at that time, needed to know what we were doing, and how they could get involved.

Ralph agreed with me and provided the magic words: "Call Linda Petrocelli in New York. She will help you." And the moment I did, things began to happen.

Linda was angelically simple in her reply. "How much do you need?" she asked. I guessed $4000 for our current projects in Ukraine. She replied with a firm "Okay!" Now, with the support of Dr. Quellhorst and Linda, financial help began to flow in.

There was support from Ukraine, at the other end of the line, as well. We invited officials from Ukraine to come to Ohio to inspect medical facilities and meet their peers in the medical profession here in the States. The Minister of Health of the Transcarpathian province of Ukraine was soon on his way, accompanied by Dr. Krusinsky, a member of the Ukrainian Parliament. They used our home in Conneaut, Ohio as their base while they toured a wide range of hospitals throughout the state and began familiarizing themselves with the political arena in Columbus.

Linda Petrocelli's confidence in our work grew in the months which followed. The two of us set a record, I think, in cutting through red tape. On one particular afternoon, I received a telephone call from Linda with a message that "a child in Yugoslavia needs a very delicate and complicated eye operation. Can you help?" I immediately phoned one of our medical contacts in Pecs, Hungary who specialized in ophthalmology and asked him if he could handle it. His answer was blunt and positive. "Get her here," he said. I called Linda back and she said she could manage it from there.

In less than ten minutes, we had cut through all the official red tape. I could not help think that this is what our ministry is all about. "We should be determined to say 'yes' to all calls for help," I thought to myself, "and work out details later."

I wanted to make our "godparent" relationship with the Ohio Conference a permanent one, so I invited Ralph to our home in Conneaut for dinner and discussions. We served him some typical Hungarian food. For starters, "hideg meggyleves", a delicious chilled soup made from sour cherries and sour cream. Following that came a plate of "paprikas csike", a combination of chicken, sour cream, tomatoes, onions, and of course some strong Hungarian paprika. This was accompanied with "galushka", small dumplings. I knew that good Hungarian food served before serious discussions always helps persuade people to consider my suggestions in a positive light. I needn't have worried, since he was already positive in agreeing to make SARA an official ministry within the Ohio Conference.

We soon found ourselves at an organizational meeting at Conference Headquarters in Columbus. I was designated Executive Director of SARA, and Dr Quellhorst graciously agreed to serve as President. Subsquently, he designed the by-laws and the organizational structure of the ministry. The Treasurer of the Ohio Conference, Cecil Easterday, agreed to handle all of the financial matters. Officially it became a not-for-profit corporation affiliated with the Ohio Conference of the United Church of Christ: a 501C3 Corporation.

This was a great blessing for me, and released a great burden from my shoulders. I have never claimed to be an accountant, let alone an administrator, but prefer to be "out and about" seeing problems at first hand and making connections to solve them. Some say that if I can't open doors, I break them down. If this were to be my epitaph some day, it would be enough.

Although he is now retired as Conference Minister, Ralph continues to expand our support base and energizes people to support SARA's projects. His wife, Sue, initiated a ministry within SARA called: SARA's Children. Let me tell you a little something about this project. When Sue Quellhorst first visited Ukraine she was immediately drawn to the great number of orphaned children in dire need of assistance. Adequate medical care and sanitation in the homes in which they were placed was barely minimal. The gypsy children were worst off. They were children born into bleakest poverty and shunned by the communities around them. They barely had enough clothes to cover their backs, and usually no shoes at all.

Sue decided to make these children, Sara's children. She began working through the Erdeyi Home in Debrecen, Hungary (similar to our Ronald McDonald houses in the US), and with the Good Samaritan Orphanage sponsored by the Hungarian Reformed Church, as well as various state-run orphanages. As a mother, she recognized the need for infant formula, toys, outdoor play equipment, sweat suits, vitamins, food supplements, clothing shoes, and specialized equipment for physically handicapped children. She also recognized a need for teachers and physical therapists

As just one example of her interest and support, over 18,000 pairs of shoes have already been transported from the United States to Sara's Children in Eastern Europe. Sue has been there. She has seen children who, as she says, "will capture your heart." She is truly a worthy godmother as she helps to "raise" SARA wth her husband. And she is available to talk to people in religious and women's organizations. Simply contact the Ohio Conference Offices of the United Church of Christ in Columbus, Ohio for more information.

Our little SARA has grown quite a bit since it was first named and "christened." I wish I had room to tell you about all of its projects throughout the world, and all the fine people who have helped and are helping in so many different ways to sustain it.. Perhaps you can get some idea from the SARA Website: www. ocucc/SARA/sara.htm.

As you look over the site you'll find that SARA is growing still bigger and more beautiful under the guidance of the current Ohio Conference Minister, The Reverend Robert Molsberry. Bob is a true friend of this ministry.

Let me tell you for a moment how SARA is already well established on the globe: our wonderful son, George, based in Hungary (and father of baby Sara after whom SARA was named) coordinates all transactions and endeavors in Eastern Europe. Drs. Donn Mettens and Alan Mikesell, as well as Alex Rovt, President of IBE Trade Corporation, are Directors for Transcarpathia, Ukraine. John Gilberg and Larry Kuhn are Directors for El Salvador. The Reverend Attila Szemesi is Director for Serbia; The Reverend Csaba Orosz for Romania. These good people are taking on great responsibilities in the areas they serve, and making great strides in improving health care for thousands of people. Many thousands!

Let me make it plain that SARA is entirely ecumenical, even though it operates under the auspices of the United Church of Christ. Our new Conference Minister, Bob Molsberry, is spearheading efforts to move SARA beyond the boundaries of the Ohio Conference into other conferences, other denominations and other countries throughout the world. Our Ecumenical Coordinator, Lana Sakash, works with people of faith from other denominations, including Lutherans and Roman Catholics. SARA serves ALL people, regardless of their nationality or faith. As a matter of fact, one of our largest contributors – we like to call them "angels" – is Jewish.

In my experience with SARA, I am amazed by the number of people who find themselves drawn to our ministry with little or no prompting and without "advertising" by us. They hear the voice of God – not necessarily our voice—and like Isaiah, they answer with the beautiful phrase from Isaiah: "Here I am Lord, send me." Let me tell you of a young lady who responded after she had asked God for a vocation. Her name was Joy Marty....

CHAPTER XVII

HOOKED ON SARA

"And I heard the voice of the Lord saying:" Whom shall I send? Then I said, "Here am I: Send me."
Isaiah 6:8 (KJV)

Joy was a young girl who lost her job in the spring of 1998 and found herself asking "why?" The "why" continued as she remained jobless throughout the summer. Then one late summer evening she found herself reading an article about SARA. The still small voice of God entered her heart and said gently: "This is why. This is why you lost your job. It opened the door for you to go free and find your calling."

She began her search by telephoning two of the people mentioned in the article – my wife, Jeannie, and myself. She told us that she wanted to use her skills as an Occupational Therapist. Could she use them to help the little children in Ukraine that she had read about?

I remember the excitement in my wife's voice when she heard this offer of a professional service that was so badly needed. Jeannie's voice rang out over the telephone lines to Joy with a very positive: "Therapist! WONDERFUL!"

We met at a UCC Church in Wakeman, Ohio, and it was love at first sight. She told me that she felt God speaking to her through our words about SARA, and that she was "hooked".

Her first trip with us followed in February, 1999. She stayed in Ukraine for over a month, and found a true passion for mission work. It turned her life around. She tells me that each time she returns to Ukraine, her heart and soul are refreshed as she reaches out to the little ones for their therapy treatments. Joy has made ten trips to Ukraine thus far and looks forward to many more. "Every time I take a child in my arms," she says, "I feel the love that is SARA."

Larry Kuhn was also "hooked." His wife, Ann, a nursery school teacher, heard about a SARA mission trip to Hungary from their Pastor. Ann's mother and father were of Hungarian descent, and she thought the trip might be a good way to "investigate her heritage. Larry was not interested. Not interested, that is, until Ann nagged him until he agreed to accompany her. Wives are like that sometimes, and all the moreso when they see a noble cause and commit themselves to it. A bit reluctantly, Larry joined the group and headed off to Hungary with them.

As part of the trip, they visited a children's home in a town called Nagydobbrony. The staff lovingly treated the children as well as they could, but there was very little in the way of facilities and equipment, and not much chance of funding to improve the situation. Ann could not help compare the spartan environment in which these children lived to conditions which little ones enjoyed in her own nursery school in New Bremen, Ohio.

Larry quickly realized the great divide between resources available in America to those in this corner of the world. He didn't need to be convinced. He was "hooked" and became an ardent supporter of SARA. Ann often tells us that "he was always a good man, but after devoting himself to the needs of the children in

Nagydobronny, he has truly become a new and finer man. How many men receive that kind of praise from their wives?

John and Joyce Gilberg heard about SARA from Larry and Ann. They were of German descent...frugal and orderly in their lives... raised five children... became leaders of their community. In due time they sold their furniture store and funeral home business and settled into a comfortable life. But through the words and actions of Larry and Ann, God managed to "hook them" as well on the SARA ministry. Since then they have visited Ukraine and El Salvador at opposite ends of the world doing good works and never missing an opportunity to tell others of the blessings which God gave them through SARA. Among other things, these four people alone solicited enough funds for the refurnishing of four ambulances. And that's just a small part of the service and long hours they have devoted to SARA.

Dr. Fleming Fallon is a Professor of Environmental health in the Graduate School of St. Joseph's College in Maine, and one of the institution's most esteemed faculty members. My wife, Jeannie, obtained her undergraduate and graduate degrees at St Joseph's and is now an adjunct instructor there. On one occasion, Jeannie and I were invited to a special presentation by Dr. Fleming who proceeded to talk about his adventures with voluntary work in Bangladesh. We invited him to dinner the next evening to elaborate on his good works there. He graciously accepted, and as he puts it, "they bent my arm with a chicken drumstick and I, too, became firmly "hooked" on SARA. Since that time, Dr Fleming has become one of SARA's firmest supporters. With expertise in public health and community medical planning, he eventually became a "natural" as President of SARA. He has covered the world with the SARA message, visiting Ukraine, Hungary, Romania, Serbia on one side of the globe, and Bolivia on the other.

People sometimes ask me how I choose people to be volunteers for SARA projects. They have it wrong. The Holy Spirit chooses them. I'm just a sinful man who prays every night for the physical strength needed to carry me on at seventy-odd years. I simply make connections between the dots in this world representing needs and resources. I like to think that God "hooks" them after I throw out the bait. And sometimes he hooks some very large fish, indeed.

A short time ago, Jeannie and I entertained a stranger in our home: a man named George Brown. George is the Community Outreach Coordinator for Ohio Senator George Voinovich. We talked with George about our experiences with Mr. Voinovich when he was Governor of Ohio This was before SARA was born… back in the early days when we first started sending medical equipment to Eastern Europe. Even then, the spirit of sharing America's resources abroad caught the attention of the Governor. His coordinator as well as his Direcetor of Health accompanied my son and I to the area in Hungary where some of the first shipments from America were arriving. The Governor himself had arranged for this load of cargo containers crammed with medical supplies. George came to see us because the Governor, now the Senator, wanted an update on the progress of this good work on which he was "hooked" so many years before. We were happy to tell him that "baby SARA" was thriving.

SARA transcends social distinctions. Because of the appeal of its message, the high and mighty are often able to **bend down** to pick up the lowly, while the lowly **reach up** with prayers and thanks that refresh and reinvigorate the givers. Let me tell you what happened in a little village in Hungary that exemplifies this.

In order to focus and facilitate our work in Eastern Europe, Jeannie and I picked a spot in Hungary just ten miles from the eastern most border of Ukraine, closeby to both the Czech Republic and Slovakia, and not all that far from Romania. In a small crossroads village called Jeke (yeah-key to American ears), we bought a small cottage with funds generously donated for that purpose by friends in Greenville, Ohio. To give you some idea of the remoteness of our "office", there is no crime in Jeke, except for a stolen bicycle now and again. The mayor is a young man, and has become a good friend of ours.

One day he came to us with a plea for help. It seems that one of the village children was diagnosed with heart disease. Her family was told that she might need a heart transplant. Can you imagine the impact on these poor peasant folk. They began to pray for a miracle. The mayor, a more practical man who realized the cost of such an operation, asked if we could assist with fund raising.

I told him we could do better than that. I immediately contacted my friend, Dr. Arpad Bellyei, the former director of the Pecs University Medical School. Arpad is "hooked" on SARA and has been from the start of the ministry. He, in turn, contacted a young and very famous heart surgeon named Dr.Lajos Pap. His reputation, I am told, is comparable to the Dubakeys and Jarviks in the medical world.

Arpad took it from there. Within hours, a young voice was talking to me as if I were his personal friend, and volunteering to come as soon as possible to Jeke. He, too, became "hooked" on SARA after hearing about its ministry and volunteered to schedule a trip with us to Ukraine to evaluate cardiac facilities there as well.

First, he came to Jeke as he promised and examined the little girl. Was it a miracle, or just Dr Pap's solid professional judgment that allowed him to tell a very relieved mother that the child's heart would heal itself as she grew a bit older, and that most likely, she would be able to lead a normal teenager's life. The entire village of Jeke rejoiced.

Dr Pap is so well known in that part of the world that when my wife Jeanne and I, together with our son, George, had lunch with him in the company of the Hungarian Consul, the owner of the restaurant thanked us for "allowing" him to serve the surgeon. This was followed by a trip to the Ukrainian border where the border crossing officials happily stopped traffic to allow our party to enter. They knew the doctor as well.

When I expressed my sincere thanks and appreciation for his time and services on behalf of SARA, Dr Pap, with much emotion, thanked ME for allowing him to participate in SARA's work. He has since told me that instead of taking his usual winter skiing trip to the Austrian Alps, he used the funds to purchase special gifts for the children at the Reformed Good Samaritan Children's Home in Nagydobronny. Although royalty has long since vanished from every country in Eastern Europe, Dr. Pap is truly a noble man in every sense of the word.

I found in my efforts with SARA that even plain, ordinary people can be just as noble in their random acts of kindess. Let me tell you about some of the many I have encountered along the way...

CHAPTER XVIII

RANDOM ACTS OF KINDESS

Matthew 25: 40 Verily I say unto you, inasmuch as ye have done it unto one of the least of these my brethren, ye have done it unto me. (KJV)

During my active ministry in congregations in Pennsylvania, Kentucky and Ohio over the past three decades -- and particularly in my work as Director of SARA -- I have always been amazed by the kind and noble acts that plain ordinary people often do for others without thought of reward or even thanks. Just out of the goodness of their hearts! I once heard these referred to as "random acts of kindness." Surely, God has a special place in Heaven for those folks who perform them.

I've told you about some of the larger acts in great detail, but let me tell you about some of the smaller ones, without elaboration, and in no particular chronological order. They are all directly related to our SARA ministry. They occurred at different times and in different places, under different, unrelated circumstances. Yet, each one of these acts made a positive impact on the lives of those touched by them. They were a tremendous blessing to those who gave them as well as those who received them. I'll let God connect the dots between these seemingly unrelated acts of kindness, and how "they made a difference."

+ Once I mentioned to a fellow pastor in Cincinnati that an orphanage in a remote part of Ukraine needed a truck…just a small one. He talked briefly with one of his parishoners and shortly thereafter we received a $5000 check in the mail. Today, this little truck operating in the "backwoods" of rural Ukraine is the only vehicle which the orphanage has to connect itself with the outside world. It makes a difference.

+There is a man names Gerald Eighmy, the owner and president of American Turned Products of Erie, PA. By some means or another, he learned that we needed a storage place for donated medical equipment that was to be shipped to eastern Europe. I received a call from him and he volunteered a portion of his building, rent free.

+A Lutheran Pastor from Wapokeneta, Ohio, who traveled with us on one of our trips to Ukraine, asked church friends who accompanied him to fill an extra suitcase with shoes for the Good Samaritan's Children's Home. He wrote later: *"When the children in the home gathered around the suitcases and tried on the shoes, I was taking pictures, and I just laughed as the children proudly showed me their new shoes. It was so exciting for all of us."*.

+The good people at St Paul's UCC in Wapakoneta, Ohio, sent a check for $6,000 to the same orphanage so that a new tractor could be purchased for the farm which produced the bulk of fresh vegetables and fruits which fed the children.

+In the city of Sremska Koumenica, Serbia, a SARA delegation delivered an assortment of medical supplies to the Institute of Oncology located in that war-weary country. Some kind and thoughtful women in America thought enough to include a quantity of wigs among the medical equipment. As Mother Theresa once said: *"We cannot do great things in this world; we can only do small things with great love."*

+In 1993, eighteen doctors and nine assistants from an association called: "VOSH --Volunteer Optometric Services to Humanity" sent a delegation to various sites in eastern Europe where they offered free eye examinations and eye care. Eventually, approximately 30,000 pairs of glasses and thousands of dollars worth of specialized medical equipment for the visually impaired were sent there. Some of the equipment is the first of its kind ever seen in that part of the world.

+On a trip to Haiti, each participant volunteered to carry two heavy boxes of badly needed detergent along with their luggage. Once again, a random act of kindness which made a vast improvement in the "ordinary living" of many, many people.

+There is an institute for handicapped and orphaned girls in Ukraine which depended upon a very small bus to handle the needs of about sixty severely impaired children. In the winter they can expect snowstorms with drifts of from three to six feet. Roads are seldom plowed, and many times the bus was sent out with a prayer that it would reach its destination. The administrator of the institute who I had met on a previous trip brought to my attention that a 25-passenger bus which was well-used, but very rugged and serviceable, could be obtained locally for the equivalent of about $2500 US dollars. I made a call to the Conference Minister of the United Church of Christ in Ohio, and he said simply: "buy it." By some means or another, he contacted an anonymous donor who put a check in the mail that very day. A random act of kindness from someone who had never been to Ukraine, but considered that a winter in Northeast Ohio was misery enough!

+Many of the gifts we receive are not random at all, but carefully thought out. A group of ladies at the North Kingsville, Ohio, Presbyterian Church heard from someone who had taken a SARA inspection trip that some orphanages in eastern Europe had only rags to cover the children in their care. As their special project, these kind women prepared a large quantity of hand-made baby quilts. This very personal gift came from their hearts as well as their hands. We made sure that photos were taken at various hospitals where babies were wrapped in these quilts, so that we could show the ladies how significant their gift was.

+During one SARA inspection visit to a hospital some years ago when life was more difficult in Ukraine, we took up a collection from among our own group and gave each of the eleven washer women in the laundry a small gift of $10 each. They sobbed their thank you for such "an enormous gift."

+Life can be dismal, and sometimes hopeless, in many of the institutions our SARA groups visit. One of the drivers who volunteered to take us around in Ukraine was named Janos. He was a short little guy who probably lived in a dingy apartment hardly bigger than a small "spare room" in Pittsburgh or Cleveland. When he heard that we were coming, he took a week's vacation from his work, without pay. Our group gathered about eighty dollars together (about two months pay for him) and tried to give it to him. He didn't want it. He was insulted that we should offer it. After all, our group was doing something good for his people. Nothing could persuade him to take money for an act of kindness and sacrifice on his part.

+Many of those to whom we give assistance want to return the favor but simply don't have the resources to do so. The field workers in a small village in El Salvador, for example, owe their supply of clean water to funds for supplies and engineers donated to SARA from individual donors in the United States and brought to them by a group of SARA volunteers. Selling fruit from their trees is one of their few means of sustenance in this villages. When our SARA group left after their project was completed, these people who were so friendly and spiritual-- but dirt poor -- willingly gave each of us a bag of jocotes (a tropical fruit) which they themselves needed to maintain a living. Today there are two clinics supplied by SARA in remote areas of this small Central American country.

+The small gypsy communities which still exist in eastern Europe are unwelcome and isolated from mainstream medical services as if they were lepers. Two physicians associated with SARA volunteered to travel to Serbia to provide a free clinic for these people who are separated from the mainstream of life.

+The Catholic Diocese of Youngstown donated funds to purchase a $2300 piece of equipment designed to enlarge the printed word. It was shipped to Hungary and now allows visually impaired children to do their homework and other reading tasks. It is the first of its kind in Hungary! It opens up a whole bright new world for these little ones.

Each of these "unrelated" acts of kindness are small, indeed, when compared with the overall needs of the world. But connected through a volunteer-driven ministry like SARA, they begin to form a global network which generates a powerful force that is not random at all, but which, like yeast, makes the bread of life rise.

I thought I might be able to prepare a list of all of those "angels" who provided donations and assistance of one kind or another since SARA was founded. I asked Jeannie to begin such a list, and she accumulated 28 pages of names from Ohio alone before I realized that it was an impossible task to identify EVERYONE here in the States and abroad who contributed some good thing, whether large or small, to help SARA grow and expand.

The examples I have given in the pages of this book are just a few of the thousands who have provided gifts of money, time and resources since SARA was born. I could not possibly list them all, but most assuredly, their names are listed in the Book of Life.

I wish I could tell you that all of our endeavors have been successful, but let me tell you about a place where our work still awaits completion...

CHAPTER XIX

CONGO COMES TO CONNEAUT

"Thou shalt love thy neighbor as thyself"
Matthew 22:39 (KJV)

I wish I could tell you that all of our SARA experiences have been success stories. Unfortunately, some are not. Sometimes political events make it nearly impossible to provide the medical assistance desperately needed. It is heartbreaking to know that millions of needy and innocent people continue to suffer as they hold out their hands to us. SARA and other ministries like it can provide much of what they need, but for reasons outside our control, it is impossible to get it to them.

In January, 1994, I received a very touching letter from Dr. Stephen Nzita Kiaku, President of the International Christian University of Zaire. Zaire is a very large country in Africa which has since been renamed: The Democratic Republic of Congo. This is what he wrote:

"Dear Brother Szilagyi,

With great interest we have heard about what God has been doing through you in Eastern Europe. We thank God for using you in such a mighty way! Glory to His Name. Africa has been violated and paralyzed by the brutality of slavery and colonization; destroyed by the complicated politics of the cold war era, and sadly forgotten during the post cold war period.. The agony in Africa continues. You, brother, do not forget us. Please help us!

While the worldwide efforts are focusing everywhere else except Africa, this is the most difficult time in its history. Many old friends have left behind a leadership vacuum and a powerless people only expecting to receive from others. Instead of giving them fish, we want to teach them to fish. This is empowering. This is the road to true freedom. This is why we have created the International Christian University of Zaire. Education is the gate to knowledge. We are seeking the help of Christians everywhere.

Please help us to help our people. We are already helping over 700 students from four African countries, both French and English speaking. Please come over and help us."

A letter like this is hard to ignore, and we set out immediately to contact Dr Kiaku and assess his needs. They were many. The university needed help training doctors. They needed almost every type of medical equipment and supplies. They needed an ambulance. And among other things, they needed a printing press to educate and communicate.

I contacted a group called the Chosen Mission Project located in nearby Eire, PA. The Executive Director, Carl Eldred, explained that they were a non-profit, charitable organization serving ecumenically in the collection and distribution of hospital equipment and medical supplies to overseas missions in economically deprived countries. Somehow or another, God always directs us to exactly the right person for the job at hand. Carl offered his help immediately and has become a great friend as well as a colleague in our plans to help the International Christian University.

As I got to know Carl better, I was amazed at the extent of the health care his association provides, ranging from rebuilding and repairing donated hospital equipment and making sure that it is compatible with the available electrical and other energy supplies. The ministry includes offering technical advice about the installation, operation and maintenance of the equipment. The Chosen group provides classes in operating room procedures and infection control in the hospital environment. Through their efforts, hospitals in economically distressed areas receive not just highly specialized equipment but the ordinary things as well, including operating tables; surgical lights; beds; gurneys; wheelchairs; crutches; and many other items.

We were so successful in gathering equipment and supplies for the International Christian University that the Zairean Ambassador to the United States, Mr. Tatanene Manata, heard about us, and expressed an interest in coming to Conneaut, Ohio, to personally receive the ambulance provided by Metro Ambulance of Cleveland. The good citizens of Conneaut even held a parade to welcome the ambassador. They were proud that a small city such as their's can have a positive impact on the international scene, and that even individuals from small communities can contribute to the improvement of medical care in other less fortunate places.

The town of about 13,000 rolled out the red carpet for the ambassador as well as other dignitaries including Dr Kiaku. A parade led the dignitaries from the American Legion Hall to Conneaut City Hall where the key to the ambulance was formally presented. Later that evening the local United Church of Christ hosted a reception for the dignitaries which was attended by hundreds.

Ambassador Manata gratefully accepted the ambulance and other medical supplies. He hoped that the Agricultural and Medical School of Ohio State University, which he visited as part of his journey to Conneaut, might consider sending professors to Zaire to teach students at the International Christian University.

We felt that SARA had made a small but important impact on medical conditions in Zaire: one which would grow and flourish in the years to come. The country is huge, after all, with a population of over 60,000,000, and a land area of about 900,000 square miles. Consider that the states of Ohio and Pennsylvania combined are about 90,000 square miles in size. We hoped that SARA might be "yeast" that would leaven the huge lump called Zaire, and that in some small way we could answer the call for help which Dr. Kiaku made to us in his eloquent letter received by us in early 1994.

However, by the end of that year, and continuing through 2008, two great civil wars have been fought within the borders of this huge country in the heart of Africa. The United Nations estimates that these wars have cost the lives of over 4,000,000 people, and that even today, about 4000 people die each week as a result of the chaos which continues. The UN reports unremitting violence: criminal activity: governmental corruption; illegal detentions: torture: kidnapping; rape; drug trafficking, murder; impressment of hundreds of children into the various rebel armies; a total lack of faith in the currency; and massive numbers of refugees scattered around the country.

Now this is not a "poor" country, as I said. It is a country rich in minerals—diamonds, gold, copper and uranium. It is a lush country which could easily feed itself and its neighbors. But political events beyond the control of its people have made them wretchedly poor and propells them in a chaotic downward spiral.

The great plans we had to provide even a limited amount of medical assistance to the people of the Congo remain unfulfilled. We cannot help but remember the letter from Dr Kiaku which said "The Agony in Africa continues." Unfortunately, it continues today even as I write these words. **It is heartbreaking.**

There have been other disappointments. Although conditions in Eastern Europe are noticeably improving, we still find small pockets of neglect left behind from the Communist regimes as we make our annual mission trips: children's homes where physical and occupational therapy is non-existent and where playground equipment and recreational opportunities are not available; hospitals where one kidney dialysis machine must serve over 1,000 patients.

We see hospitals newly opened which already have cracked walls and where there is no lighting in the stair wells. We see very old hospitals where the surgical suites were equipped in 1938! Treatable and terminal diseases often go undetected because of the lack of equipment and supplies.

We see frustration in the eyes of physicians trying to handle medical problems with little or no equipment, and who do not always have the latest medical training and expertise which is commonplace in the United States. But at least in Europe, we find more and more governmental recognition of the problems and a willingness to "fix things."

SARA tries to meet immediate needs at every place our delegations visit. Our efforts to bring medical assistance and to cultivate education are endless, but they continue. This is why we spend much of our time bringing physicians to the United States so that they can study here and carry back their knowledge to their own countries – and train others in those countries in the skills and techniques which they have learned.

The plea for help from Africa still rings in our ears. Perhaps an upcoming election will provide encouragement for the future. You can be sure that when some semblance of order and stability returns to that land, SARA will be there to help.

CHAPTER XX

A CHILDREN'S SERMON FOR ADULTS

"Suffer the little children and forbid them not to come unto m: for as such is the kingdom of heaven."
Matthew 19:14 (KJV)

At every congregation I served, either my wife, Jeannie, or I delivered a "children's sermon" as part of the Sunday service. Sometimes we presented these sermons in the form of a fairy tale, and as you know, all fairy tales begin with…

ONCE UPON A TIME, in a city in Ukraine named Uzgorod, there lived seven nuns in a small cottage at the edge of town who were dedicated to good works and who lived in poverty. Six of the nuns spent each of their days in nursing the sick and helping the poor in all kinds of ways throughout the city, while the seventh--called Sister Ludmilla—spent her days in begging for food, clothes and whatever else could be used to ease the lives of the needy people in that city.

When Sister Ludmilla and the other nuns arrived home each evening, tired and weary, they placed everything which she had gathered on a large wooden table so that they could look through it and decide where it was needed most. Naturally, their own needs were the least and the last served.

They made packages of food and sorted all the clothes by age and size. On the next day, they distributed these packages to families with the greatest need. They set aside for themselves just a few scraps of bread and cheese and perhaps a potato or two. They placed these in a small wooden box which they kept in their tiny kitchen.

In the summer they usually had an abundance of vegetables and even a few eggs left by the villagers on their front steps. At Eastertime, a small ham might mysteriously appear, left by one of the more prosperous farmers in the area. But in the winter their dinners were sparse indeed. Still, they said their prayers over potato soup as if it were a banquet, and they depended upon God to supply their needs from day to day.

One morning in the coldest part of winter when the sun had not yet risen, Sister Ludmilla greeted the sisters with a message of gloom. "There is a large hole in the wooden box where last evening's bread was stored," she said. " and I believe we will have no breakfast this morning." The nuns concluded, quite rightly, that the rats had found their way to the food, and they agreed that, it being such a cold winter, the poor animals had to eat as well as they did. But it was a struggle to go out into the cold that morning without a crumb to eat, and they were fearful about storing other food in the cottage.

Besides all that, there was a hole in the roof where the snow came in (and no doubt where the rats came in as well), and there was a broken window pane where the wind whistled. The patched the hole with a piece of cardboard which certainly didn't do much to keep the heat in. The fireplace smoked a great deal and there is no doubt that it needed to be cleaned. But they had no skills to handle all of this. They doubted very much that they could carry on their work in the village if help did not arrive around Eastertime..

While begging at the town's hospital the next day, Sister Ludmilla heard the nurses talking about some medical equipment they had received from the United States. It was not new equipment, but it was better than anything the hospital had ever had, and it could be used to help dozens, perhaps hundreds of patients for many years to come.

"Who sent you this from America?", she asked politely, and was told that SARA had sent it. "SARA must be a fine Christian woman given to such good works," she thought. She had no doubt that the hand of God was in her works and that if she knew of their plight, she might be willing to help them as well.

So she asked for the address of this good woman named Sara. The nurses laughed. "SARA is not a woman," they said. "It is an organization and it is based in a city in the United States called Conneaut in the state of Ohio. Now that struck a note with Sister Ludmilla because her uncle had left for America many years before and had settled in this place called Ohio where he became a steel worker. He had long since been called to the Lord, but surely God was giving her a sign that help lay ahead.

That evening as the sisters gathered for a meager supper, Sister Ludmilla asked Sister Olga to write a letter (because she was the most studious one among the seven). Sister Olga took some paper from the kitchen cabinet where they stored such things, and began to write. It explained who they were and how they needed just a few things to keep them going until Easter time when the weather would clear up. They needed these few things, she wrote, so that they could continue to help the poor people in Uzgorod. She ended the letter with these simple words: "Please help us".

She addressed it to the Director of SARA and wrote very carefully the address on the envelope which was going to this magical place in Ohio. All seven nuns gave a blessing to the note, and early the next morning, Sister Ludmilla delivered it to the postmaster and explained that she was sending for help to America. Since she had never mailed a letter to a place so far away before, she was astounded by the price of the stamps. Overwhelmed! But the postmaster was so moved that he paid for the postage himself, stamped it with authority and sent the letter on its way. The nuns prayed for a fast delivery, since time was running out.

In due time, the Director of SARA received this strange little note and immediately shared it with his wife, Jeannie. After reading it he said: "There is nothing we can do about this. We deal only with medical needs and hospital supplies. Besides all that, this is a church matter, and we aren't even Catholic. I doubt that anyone would listen to us."

His wife thought about it for a moment and then said: "Why don't we just send an email around to all of our friends, asking them if they would like to help, and then just wait and see what happens."

This they did, and within two days – on Good Friday – a telephone call came from a good friend: a good man; a righteous Jew called Alex. "How much do you need?" he asked. You see, by coincidence, Alex was born in a town very close to Uzgorod. At the beginning of the next week, just after Easter, a check was received at SARA Headquarters from Alex payable to **"SARA for the Nuns."**

In the meantime, another friend of SARA, a Monsignor in Cleveland, was called and asked if he could inquire as to whether these people in Uzgorod were who they said they were.

And now a long sequence of miracles occurred. Monsignor passed the word along to someone who passed it along to someone else, who eventually passed it along to a Bishop in Munkacs which was very near Uzgorod. The nuns were indeed "real", and word went back to SARA that help was on its way. Not only would they receive a new wooden box to hold their food, but once the

Bishop learned that help was coming from America, he was not to be undone. He announced that the nuns would be supplied with additional food and supplies; their cottage would be renovated; their windows replaced; their fireplace cleaned; and things made right all around.

The nuns were overjoyed. You see, in their simple way they knew that when they prayed the words: **"Give us this day our daily bread"**, God would surely answer them. The fact that a righteous Jewish man who they did not know; who was born near Uzgorod, and now lived thousands of miles away; sent them help which arrived at Eastertime –just as they prayed it would – was not as astonishing to them as it was to others who heard their story.

Most fairy tales are made-up stories called allegories. That is to say, the stories never really happened, but they could have.

But in this case, the story of the seven nuns in the far-off city of Uzgorod; the "miraculous" benevolence of a righteous Jewish man named Alex Rovt who sent help coincidentally on Good Friday; and the response of the good Bishop during Easter Week is not a fairy tale. Everything happened the way you have heard it.

It's quite simple. There was a great need in a far away place. A short letter explained that need to someone who cared enough to respond. Emails were sent like messengers (angels perhaps) in the night, and help arrived just where and when it should have. Even the Director of SARA and his wife were surprised and delighted that they had played a small part in this "miracle."

That's the children's sermon for the day, and every word is true.

CHAPTER XXI

A PARABLE FOR TODAY: THE LIFEGUARD WHO WASN'T WATCHING

And he spake many things unto them in parables
Matthew 13:3 (KJV)

I often used simple little stories in my sermons with a "point" that people could easily understand and remember. I took my lead from Jesus who used parables in much of his teaching. He delivered them by word of mouth to crowds who gathered in the meadows and on the hillsides, or beside the sea, to listen to them. And that's the way these people passed them along to others. By word of mouth. Not written down, because most of these good folks were illiterate.

They never attended a school. They never read a book because there were neither books nor schools available to them.

To get his point across, Jesus placed his stories in familiar settings: a sheep pen; a barley field; or the shade of a fig tree. He included images of common ordinary things that these simple folks knew about: wheat stalks; thorn bushes; mustard seeds. Occasionally he included images of things they could only dream about, such as pearls of great price.

Often, Jesus caught his listeners by surprise when a despised Samaritan became the hero of the story, while a high born traveler who should have known better passed by a wounded man lying on the side of the road. Without even a glance! Even today we can create mental pictures of "The Prodigal Son", "An Old Woman Searching for a Lost Coin," and "The Lost Sheep". All these stories remain as luminous pictures in our minds more than 2000 years after the telling of them.

I wonder how many people will remember the television programs and movies filled with sex and violence which we see today after the next 2000 years have passed?

Sometimes Jesus added an explanation at the end of the Parable to make the meaning clearer. Sometimes he didn't need to, because the meaning was quite clear: **A rich man ignores a poor man starving on the front steps of his house. Why is he surprised by his fate when he dies?** At any rate, the parables were so effective that the simple country people passed them along to the next generation by memory and word of mouth for several hundred years or so until the words were finally written on parchment and turned into what we now call: The New Testament.

Now I propose to tell you a "parable for today," and I promise to supply an explanation at the end of the story just in case you miss the point.

A man was on vacation on a beautiful summer afternoon in Highland Lake, New Jersey, and decided that it was a fine day to take a swim. He walked down to the beach and sat on a blanket for a moment to enjoy the sun. "What a great day to be alive," he thought, and he thanked God quietly, as was his custom.

The beach was "guarded" by a young, suntanned lifeguard sitting on one of those high chairs where he had a full view of the lake. From the looks of him, he was probably going to be playing fullback at one of the local colleges within a few weeks. Perhaps

Rutgers, or Princeton. He had the look of a young man who was quite comfortable "in his skin" and in his job, and prepared to meet any crisis which might arise during his watch.

The trouble was that he was not watching very carefully. For one thing, his ears were plugged into a small radio with a very large sound. For another thing, he was reading a magazine about racing cars rather than giving full attention to what was happening on a large raft about fifty yards from the beach. The raft served as a warning that this was as far from the beach as swimming was permitted.

And what WAS happening on the raft?

It appeared to the man on the blanket that a middle-aged gentleman who was clinging to the rope ladder on one side of the raft was acting very strangely. He seemed to be trying to climb up the rest of the way, but not making much progress. It was hard to tell from that distance.

The man on the beach walked over to the guard and waved his hand to get his attention. "That man out there seems to be in some sort of trouble," he said.

"What?" said the lifeguard, while he lifted one side of his ear plugs. "The man on the raft," repeated the man. "He doesn't look right to me!" "Look right? What do you mean, "look right?" The lifeguard cast a glance toward the raft.

"He seems to be trying to climb up the rope ladder," but getting nowhere," said the man on the beach.

The lifeguard glanced toward the raft again with a hand cupped over his eyes. "He looks okay to me. Maybe just showin' off a bit. He's certainly not in any danger of drowning. If he were in the water I'd be concerned. But he's hanging on tight to the ladder."

The man started back to his blanket, but then turned around and called out once more to the lifeguard: "Look", he said, "Will you do me a favor?"

"Huh", grunted the lifeguard, lifting both earplugs.

"Will you do me a favor? Can we swim together out there and see if he's okay?" The lifeguard answered in a grumble: "Look, mister. I don't want to embarrass him!"

The man on the beach pondered that and then said: "Why don't we pretend to have a race, and when we get to the raft we won't embarrass him if nothing's wrong."

"A race!" laughed the lifeguard.

The man on the beach surmised at that moment that the lifeguard was probably on the swimming team at Princeton. Probably their best swimmer. But he persisted. "Yes, I know you'll get there first, and if you do and there's nothing wrong…well…then nothing's lost. But if there IS something wrong, pull him up onto the raft right away."

"Okay," said the lifeguard reluctantly. "But I know he's okay. He's not acting like something's really wrong."

The man and the lifeguard stood at the edge of the lake, and then ran into the water together. Naturally, the lifeguard outpaced him from the start. He was ten yards ahead in the blink of an eye. But the man on the beach – now the man in the water – made steady progress. As he neared the raft, the muscular lifeguard had already grabbed the man under the arms and pulled him quickly atop the raft.

"I think he's having a stroke or something," yelled the lifeguard. "You wait here with him and I'll swim back for help."

In about ten minutes, a fire truck arrived and soon they had a boat out to the raft and the stricken man in an ambulance bound for the hospital. He had, indeed, suffered a slight stroke and soon would have lost his grip and slipped under the water. He survived.

The man on the beach, who was now the man on the raft, sat with his feet dangling in the water to regain his composure (and his breath) while the emergency rescue proceeded.

He thought to himself: **This lifeguard is just like most Americans, sitting comfortably in their high chairs overlooking the world. They are all well fed, healthy, and well muscled. They are compassionate and caring people who, once in action, sincerely want to help those less fortunate than themselves. They cannot begin to understand the depth of all the problems out there in countries which are less fortunate than their own. But they know about some of the problems, and they know that there are plenty of resources over here in the USA to correct them.**

But there is no one to point the way and to stimulate them to action. And the culture of the day distracts them.

SARA IS LIKE THE MAN ON THE BEACH. It is a facilitator and sometimes an agitator. It steps into situations on a personal basis: face to face with the needy, where governments and even churches are sometimes unable to penetrate. It reaches down to the common person, figures out the problem; directs attention to it; and begins working on it from bottom up. It has no resources of its own, but recognizes that untapped resources are available in abundance in America, **if only someone asks.** SARA and other groups like it are very small organizations in the scheme of things which are waiting to be asked.

This is a parable for today. Think about it. Perhaps it explains a little better the reason why SARA was founded and its purpose in the Twenty-First Century World. Perhaps you can find it in your heart to get involved with organizations like this, or similar projects in your church or synagogue.

People sometimes ask me whether Jesus "made up" these parables, or whether they were true stories that actually occurred during his itinerate preaching along the dusty roads or by the Sea of Galilee.

I can assure you that this story about the lifeguard is true, because I was the man on the beach in New Jersey many years ago. The actual rescue work was done by others. I simply pointed out the problem and persisted with a plea for action. My wife tells me that I am a very stubborn man, and I suppose I am.

May I ask you to be stubborn, too, when you see a need that might be met or a problem which might be solved by your calling attention to it. Please pass along the message in his parable to others. Use your fax or email. Or simply spread the message by word of mouth.

It worked for Jesus.

CHAPTER XXII

SO THIS IS RETIREMENT

"Then said I, Lord, how long?"
Isaiah 6:11 (KJV)

I'm sitting in my living room on a snowy March day thinking about my 73rd birthday which is coming up before the end of the month. Seventy-three years is a lot of years, but not so many. I have a friend who is my same age visiting with me today. We talk about our ailments. I tell him that I have pains in my legs. He says to me: "I do, too, if I think about it. So let's not think about it."

I've been retired from active ministry at my church in Conneaut, Ohio for over a decade. But despite a few minor ailments, my life is full to overflowing, and with SARA, my work is never finished. This is my schedule for today:

We have a mother and a daughter staying with us until April 20. The daughter was operated on for scoliosis in March and has been staying with us during her recovery: a sweet girl who we happened upon in Turkey last year.

As Jeannie and I walked together in a small Turkish town on a very warm summer evening, I passed a young girl and her family. She was about sixteen and a very pretty girl. But I noticed that she wore a heavy black shawl, even though the weather was hot and humid, and it appeared as if she were hiding something under it. I immediately guessed that she probably had a deformity.

As I've told you before, people in Eastern Europe have a tendency to believe that a deformity is a disgrace. And so they hide their impaired children away, or cover them when they go out with them.

I immediately approached the family, and asked them their nationality. They were Russian, but the girl answered me in English. I recognized her deformity as I drew closer. Scoliosis! A large hump on her back pulled her into a agonizingly bent position. She was walking crab-like, rather than with normal, straight steps. I said to the girl: "We can help you. We can make you straight."

I'm sure her family wondered what I was saying, and the girl was quite naturally frightened. She told me later that she thought I was crazy. Well, that would not be the first time someone accused me of that.

I immediately began to speak in Russian to her parents. I gave them my card and explained who I was and what SARA represented. And I told them that we could help the girl –Svetlana was her name – and make her whole again. I gave them names of agencies in Ukraine and Russia to call if they needed information about me or about SARA. And I told them I would be in Turkey a few more days if they wished to contact me. I gave them my phone number at our hotel.

Two days passed, and we heard nothing. We would be leaving for Hungary on the third day before noon. Suddenly, the phone rang, and the rest is another miracle made in the name of SARA.

After some complicated maneuvering, we managed to get both Svetlana and her Mother to the United States. The girl was operated on at Shriners Hospital in Erie, PA, and she is now convalescing in our home in Conneaut. She will remain with us through the end of April. And she will walk straight and unashamed when she returns home.

But it isn't all that easy. She is recuperating well enough, but she could recover more quickly if she exercised more. Her mother wants to keep her in bed most of the time and she coddles her. What Mother wouldn't, after what her child has been through? So today I have to speak to her like a "Dutch Uncle" and lay down some hard rules. She will have to walk more, and continue her exercises. She cannot spend her day in bed. Otherwise she is likely to get pneumonia or suffer a blood clot.

I spoke to her this morning-- rather harshly I'm afraid-- in Russia, and explained that she would have to get "up and around." Her mother nods, but only half agrees, I think. It's human nature to coddle a sick child, and to settle for a posture which is "almost perfect" after years of walking sideways like a crab. Just a bit more exercise, and she will stand straight as a tree trunk. I must explain this to her, and it is difficult, because I do not suffer her pain. I have only a few leg pains that I can dismiss by not thinking too hard about them.

My friend, Art, who is my same age, is having lunch with us today, but first I have an interview with a local newspaperman –Mark Todd from the Conneaut Star Beacon. He wants a few facts about my life and about my wife who has just earned an honorary doctorate from The Surgical and Pediatric Association of Transcarpathia, Ukraine.

I want very much for people to know more about my wife, Jeannie, who has been my brains and my strength from the moment we set out on the SARA ministry. She is the housekeeper who tends to the needs of the children and their parents who live within our household while they are recuperating. As a registered nurse in her own right, she tends to their medical needs and aids in their recovery. She schedules all of my appointments and keeps me faithful to them. She sees that all the bills are paid.

She maintains the network that connects me with hundreds of our personal contacts throughout the world. She does this through the medium of the internet which is a Godsend to our work. As for me, the internet remains a mystery. I don't even want to step close to it. But Jeannie understands it and works through it to help me accomplish whatever needs to be done, whether it be in Eastern Europe, Congo, El Salvador, wherever. The internet can reach into the most intimate corner of every home. In that respect it's frightening and can be used for the worst of reasons. But we have great respect for the good it can do, and Jeannie uses it constantly to send messages and receive information from people far beyond our borders.

Sometimes we receive message of despair and disappointment which go straight to our hearts, such as the message received from Dr. Kiaku.

As the interview with Mark Todd continues, my friend Art joins in the conversation and tells the newspaperman a few details about my pastorate in his hometown of Millvale, PA, back in the 1980's. Those were happy days, watching my three children grow up and working within a family-type church where everyone was related to one another. Art has a good memory, and reminds me of things that I had long forgotten. He wants to write a book about me, and more importantly, about all the things, good and bad, and sometimes horrible, that happened to me in the past seventy-three years which ultimately led to the birth of SARA.

We will talk more over lunch, but now I have to answer several phone calls and handle details about shipping medical supplies; thanking benefactors (we are a strictly volunteer organization); and discussing details of our trip to Hungary and Ukraine in April. I also need to call the Office of the Ohio Conference of the

United Church of Christ which has taken SARA into its heart and supports it in so many ways.

Mark Todd and Art have been waiting patiently for me to finish several multi-lingual telephone conversations. Mark asks if I ever dreamt that SARA would become so widespread and all-encompassing. After all, it began rather simply as a source of information about scoliosis and as a distributor of basic medical supplies to Hungary. Now it covers much more. Besides tracking down and shipping more sophisticated equipment to Eastern Europe and other parts of the world, SARA also supplies medical treatment for children such as Svetlana, and educates qualified doctors in the United States who carry their knowledge back to their own countries. I told Mark that I knew from the start that it would be a success, and eventually would outgrow our humble beginnings.

Now children come to SARA for treatment of all manner of medical problems, including major plastic surgery for cleft palates, hare lips, and serious burns. When we go to Europe, we visit mental hospitals and orphanages to see first hand where we can lend a hand. SARA has provided eyeglasses and eye operations to entire villages. It has provided equipment and technicians to improve dental hygiene. On one of our trips to Ukraine, for example, we carried a portable dental unit as part of our luggage.

And speaking of trips, we will be making our next one in a few weeks. There are so many things to do before we leave: checking on supplies; making contacts on our side and on the European side to assure that everyone is on the same schedule and that facilities are prepared to meet us. Dignitaries have to be notified and scheduled. Doctors going with us need to have complete information about who they will meet; what they will teach and where they will operate from. There will be speeches to give; volunteers to be found: a thousand and one things to do.

I had a mild heart attack last December. Everyone tells me that I must "slow down", but when I look out at the thousands of people who need our help, I realize that the world will not "slow down" to help them. If SARA does not help them, who will?

My reward is not monetary. My reward is having a smiling Ukrainian grandmother clasp my hand and bless me for helping her grandchild walk straight again; or a border guard making way for me through customs and yelling at everyone in sight: "This is Szilagyi. He's the one who brought eye glasses for our whole village."

My reward is seeing a poor boy with a crooked spine smile again, despite all of the pain and suffering endured through several major operations. He smiles because he knows that when he returns home, the other boys will not make fun of him, or ignore him because he walks "funny" and cannot ride a bicycle. And Svetlana, who could barely walk when we found her on a side-street in Turkey, will not only walk straight, but will dance with some fine young man one day. I smile to think of it.

At age 73, I no longer serve a church with an active ministry as a Pastor. But I continue to serve where I can through my work with SARA, and on a personal basis with people in the Conneaut community who have a need for someone to talk and share with them.

There was an old woman named Minnie who lived on a street nearby, and with whom I shared some of my time nearly every other day or so. Minnie was ninety-three, and she was Jewish. But with her European background and because of my personal experiences with many fine Jewish people, we were able to tell stories together, laugh together, and even pray together. I visited with her several times during her last stay in the hospital, and she was courageous and righteous to the end. Imagine my surprise, when the administrator of the hospital showed me the top page of the file which Minnie had completed when she was admitted. She indicated that her religion was Jewish. She noted as her pastor: Reverend Steve Szilagyi.

My friend Art left for Pittsburgh after lunch. He has the job of taking the many, many pages about my life and my experiences with SARA, condensing them, and putting them into the form of neat chapters. He knows I have a very busy day ahead of me. He tells me that I am a "Peripatetic Pastor", a big word which is Greek to me. But he says that it means, in essence, a Pastor to the World. What a grand title for an immigrant born in a time of chaos with no real direction in life: A homeless boy who wandered through Europe in his adolescent years. Somehow, God gave him a direction, and he found himself moving within a force called SARA. With God's help it continues to flow unabated as it strives to serve suffering humanity.

But I must sign off for now. I have many things to do before setting off for Hungary. If you want to come along on one of our trips, you're more than welcome to do so. We are in constant need of volunteers and medical equipment and supplies of all kinds. And I guarantee that you will quickly forget your own pains and infirmities when you see for yourselves the thousands out there who are far more worse off than you could ever imagine. Things are getting better in that part of the world, but there is still much to do.

God continues to call us, and we must answer as in Isaiah 6: "Here I am, Lord, send me." And when we begin to puff ourselves up and congratulate ourselves on what "we" have accomplished, He reminds us in a gentle hymn: "For THINE is the glory."

God bless us all. And when we ask God: "How long until we can stop giving," know that the answer is: **When He stops giving to us."**

CHAPTER XXIII -- EPILOGUE

SO MUCH FOR RETIREMENT!

"Bear ye one another's burdens, and so fulfill the law of Christ"
Galatians 6: 2(KJV)

I thought I was ready for retirement last year at age 73. But now I'm 74, and just returned from a SARA inspection trip to Hungary and Ukraine, and never felt better in my life. I have already forgotten the pains and infirmities of 2007 and look forward to continuing my efforts with SARA in 2008 and 2009 and 2010, and why not beyond, as far as God wills it.

While there is still much to be done, it was gratifying during my trip in May and June of this year to see that Eastern Europe has come a long way in the past sixteen years. The governments are more stable and the people see progress being made. There is no doubt that a better life lies ahead for regions which have been oppressed and brutalized throughout most of the 20th Century. Best of all, the good works which SARA initiated sixteen years ago continue to increase and bear fruit.

All the places we visited this Spring, including Good Samaritan Children's Home in Ukraine, the Regional Children's Hospital and St. Michael's Orphanage in Munkacs, to mention just a few, are thriving and expanding their services to their communities. These are institutions which I'm proud to say have been vigorously supported by SARA in terms of supplying medical equipment; training and making available physicians; as well as providing financial assistance. The efforts made are truly ecumenical, with a blessed mixture of good will and hard work from Protestant, Roman Catholic and Orthodox sources.

There are always small but meaningful rewards in the work which we do. But sometimes there are big ones! I received a big one on July 8, 2008 when I was called to the Ukrainian Embassy in Washington DC and honored with a medal! Ukrainian Ambassador to the United States, Dr. Olan Shamshur, said it was for the medical missions of mercy that have improved the lives and the health of many thousands of people in his country, and for making a "significant personal contribution to the strengthening of Ukraine's history and cultural heritage." Imagine that! I am receiving a medal for doing something which I love doing and which has enriched my life far more than anything I could possibly do for others.

I must tell you a little bit about the medal. It was authorized by President Viktor Yushchenko – a hero in his own right. It is reserved for "renowned state, political and public figures," and is the highest civilian honor bestowed by the Ukraine. How proud my wife and family were to see it presented to me at ceremonies in the Ukrainian Embassy. And yet, mixed with pride, I find myself thinking of words in Galatians 6 which I have always tried to live by: *"God forbid that I should glory, save in the cross of our Lord Jesus Christ."* These are the words which bring me down to earth and set me to continue my tasks on behalf of SARA.

How easily we can use a medal or a grand reward of one kind or another to puff ourselves up and seek special treatment and favors. As I see it, it should be the other way around. The medal should be used as a special key to open more doors and cut through more red tape in order to reach the sick and needy who still stand waiting at the gate. They are like Lazarus in the Bible who sat at the door of the rich merchant, hoping for relief but not expecting very much.

I am somewhat notorious now as a representative of the blessed SARA ministry who knocks doors down if he can't open them. I cannot tell you how many times I am approached in Eastern Europe by poor folks who recognize me and hesitantly ask for small favors on behalf of their families. No one is ever turned away. Some time ago, I met an employee of on of our hospitals who walked with a severe limp and in great pain. He was embarrassed to ask for help for himself. But we interceded and arranged for him to have hip surgery. When I visited the same hospital in March, the fellow ran up to me. He pulled a photo from his wallet. "Look at this," he said with one of the widest smiles I have ever seen. "Look at my leg! This is me, kicking a football to my son."

SARA's good reputation helps me to cross international borders with a simple wave of the hand to arrange the swift distribution of equipment, supplies and medical workers from "where it's at" to "where it's needed."

At one point during my visit this Spring, we had surgical procedures looming for children with hare lips, cleft palates, and caved-in chests as well as scoliosis. Knowledge in the area of plastic surgery, orthopedics, and pediatrics –all three—were required. So we arranged for three physicians from three different countries to cooperate in scheduling and performing the operations. I call it "an exchange of brains", and it would not have been possible in the "not so long ago" when there were closed and heavily guarded borders, as well as excessive red tape. SARA transcends both politics and borders, and the work is done.

It's my firm opinion that many of the problems facing the world today, and not only in the United States but in all countries, cannot be solved by political action alone. Only through the compassionate and unselfish work of ministries such as SARA. We are trusted because the border guards and the state police and the politicians observe our unselfish acts of mercy on behalf of the people, and they react with openness and thankfulness rather than suspicion and obstruction.

Let me give you an example of an impossible international situation which will never be solved through political solutions or by military actions. We receive emails from all parts of the world asking for help, and none more poignant than those coming from Zimbabwe in southern Africa. I heard on television earlier this week that inflation has become so severe that the value of one US dollar is equal to thirty billion Zimbabwe dollars. Those who seek help from SARA have no resources whatsoever. They ask for bandages, Non-perscription drugs, and the simplest of medical supplies to provide some small comfort to a people spiraling into chaos. If they had money to pay for these things a few months ago, they could not in their wildest imagination pay for them now. All savings and pocket money is valueless. The government currently in control does not permit direct assistance from western countries who they consider "colonial masters." Hopefully they will respect the humanitarian offerings of groups like SARA, and perhaps SARA's small efforts may open a wider crack in the door. We will try. We continue to try.

A boy in Transcarpathia has been diagnosed with a rare and incurable type of cancer, so we call the Ohio State University Medical Center in Columbus and see if anything can be done. Another cancer patient in the same city needs a special drug. So we call a pharmacy in Vienna, Austria, and the drug is delivered to him, The Mayor of one of the Ukrainian cities we visit has a small son has suffered from epileptic seizures for over six years. So we arrange a consultation and examination by specialists in Hungary. Some Gypsy children shunned by the community are badly in need of dental care. We round up three dentists and ask them to go over to the camp and do as much as they can to help. They agree, and life in a poor, wretched community is suddenly greatly improved. Their children smile again. In other words, SARA does what it can and somehow God connects the dots for us.

Of course I am proud to have received a medal for my work with SARA, but I can't help thinking about how many hundreds of heroic souls have worked with us since 1992 without being officially recognized. Let me give you an example of just one. His name is Jim Taraczkozy. He lives a quiet life in the little town of Conneaut Lake, Pennsylvania. For many, many years he has volunteered to drive his truck all over Pennsylvania and Ohio to pick up medicines, clothes, baby supplies, medical equipment and anything else donated for use by SARA. Jim and his wife of 44 years don't have much money, but very big hearts. They even hosted three children from Transcarpathia and Serbia who came to the US for medical attention. Tom will never get a medal. He doesn't expect one. But he is content--and very pleased—by my referring to him as "SARA's Transportation Director".

One final word about medals. Following the presentation in Washington DC someone in the audience said to me: "You realize of course that this is the highest reward you will ever receive." My answer was one which calls me from retirement whenever I think about it, and which keeps me involved as much as I'm able to in the ongoing work of SARA. It is simply this: "My highest reward is yet to come."

What better ending can there be to a book, or to any life, for that matter.